Little Pilgrim's Progress

Little Pilgrim's Progress

Illustrated by
W. Lindsay Cable

Helen L. Taylor

From John Bunyan's classic work

MOODY PRESS
CHICAGO

ISBN 0-8024-4926-3

15 17 19 20 18 16 14

Printed in the United States of America

Preface

Although *The Pilgrim's Progress* is read with delight by hundreds of children, few of them, probably, are able to grasp more than a faint idea of its meaning. The "dark and cloudy words," which "do but hold the truth, as cabinets enclose the gold," are quite beyond their comprehension; and, to the young mind, the record of Christian's pilgrimage is attractive simply as a story of adventure, and its perusal affords infinite pleasure, but not much profit.

If John Bunyan were alive at the present time, I think he would forgive me for the liberty I have taken in attempting to unlock his treasury and to bring "that gold, those pearls, and precious stones" a little nearer to the childish hands, which are always so ready to receive such gifts.

I am glad to find that, as a serial, my story has given pleasure to the readers of *Sunday*; and I trust that, in its present form, it may prove equally acceptable to other children.

PART 1

LITTLE PILGRIM'S PROGRESS

1

Little Christian Hears of the Celestial City

*L*ittle Christian lived in a great city called Destruction. Its streets were full of boys and girls who laughed and played all day long. This was in the summertime when the sun was shining and the city looked bright and pleasant. On the rainy days in winter the children did not feel so happy, and they would sometimes be glad to sit down quietly and listen to stories.

Now and then a grave-looking man, or a woman with a gentle face, would come to the city for a little time, and these strangers always tried to make friends with the children, and were willing to tell them stories whenever they would listen.

"There is a beautiful country," they would say, "far away from this city. A very good and wise King rules over it, who loves little children dearly. The Prince to whom your city belongs is wicked and cruel, and he hates our good King. But one day an army will come from the King's country to fight against your Prince, and this city will be burned, and all the people in it will be killed."

Then the children asked, "What will become of us?"

And the strangers always answered, "You must leave this city now, while you are young and strong, and travel to the King's country. In the Celestial City where He lives you will be quite safe."

Little Christian heard this many times, and he often thought about it; but whenever he said to his playfellows, "Shall we go to the Celestial City?" they laughed at him and told him that it was only a make-believe story about the King, and that no city could be better or safer than their own.

But little Christian felt quite sure that the strangers had spoken the truth; and one day he found an old Book, in which were written the very same things about the King and the Celestial City and their own wicked Prince and his city, which would certainly be burned when the King came.

He showed the Book to his companions, but they laughed all the more and said, "That Book was written hundreds of years ago. It is of no use now. The King's army has never come, and very likely it never will. At any rate we may as well play as long as we can."

But little Christian did not want to play. He felt tired and unhappy, and he sat down and wondered whether he could find the way to the Celestial City by himself. He was such a little boy that he was afraid he might be lost if he tried to make a long journey alone. He opened his Book again, and he read a beautiful story in it about the King's own Son, who had once visited the City of Destruction and had spoken kindly to the boys and girls in the streets, saying, "[Let] the little children . . . come unto me."

If He were only here now, thought little Christian, *perhaps He would take me back with Him; but I could never go all that long, long way alone!*

Then the tears came into his eyes and rolled down his cheeks. They fell upon his clothes, and as he brushed them away he saw how soiled and dusty his little suit had become. He had worn it a long time, and he had played so much that the cloth was getting quite thin and shabby. This added to his sadness, for he thought that if he *did* find his way to the Celestial City, his clothes would be worn out long before he got there, and how could he expect the King to receive a little boy dressed in nothing but rags?

At last he took up his Book and went home, and his nurse wondered why he looked so tired and sad. He told her that he would like to go to the Celestial City; but she laughed, as his playmates had done, and said, "You are a silly boy. There is no Celestial City. If you go wandering along the roads after those strangers you will get lost."

So little Christian went to bed and cried until he fell asleep.

2

Little Christian Is Found by Evangelist

*W*hen little Christian went out the next morning the sun was shining and his companions were running about. They called to him to join them; but he said, "I cannot play. I think we ought to start on our journey."

"What a foolish boy you are," they cried, "to be always talking about that Celestial City! You had better go and look for it instead of crying up and down and spoiling all our fun."

So they ran away, and little Christian stayed by himself.

Presently Christiana came down the street with her baby sister. She had been standing by when the boys had laughed at Christian the day before, and she had felt very sorry that he should be teased. Christian liked Christiana, and he was glad to see her coming.

She stopped to speak to him.

"You are crying again, little Christian! You should not listen to what the strangers say if it makes you so unhappy. Come into the fields, and we will make daisy chains for baby."

Little Christian thought he would like that. Christiana was gentle, and though she did not believe the stories he had told her out of his Book, she never teased him as the boys did.

"You know," he said, as they walked along, "I *must* go to the King, because I have a burden to carry, and no one but He can take it from me."

"Where is your burden?" asked Christiana.

"It is on my back, and it feels so heavy that it makes me too tired to play."

Christiana looked very grave. "I think you must be ill, little Christian, if you fancy such things. You haven't any burden on your back."

"Ah," said the little boy, "*you* cannot see it, but I can feel that it is there, and I shall always be tired until it is gone."

The three children stayed in the fields and were very happy together; but when Christian went home at night he began to think of the Celestial City again and fretted until his nurse was quite angry with him. He had no kind mother to love and comfort him, and his father was one of the great men of the city and had no time to notice his little boy.

Christian hoped that he would meet Christiana again in the morning; but she was busy at home, and the other boys and girls would have nothing to do with him, because they said he was dull and stupid and could not play properly. So he wandered off into the fields by himself and sat down upon a bank to think. After a while he heard a step near to him, and looking up he saw one of the strangers on his way to the city—a man with a grave and pleasant face, whose name was Evangelist. He had seen little Christian before, and he turned aside to speak to him.

"What are you crying for?" he asked, for there were tears in the child's eyes.

Little Christian felt so comforted by the sound of his gentle voice that he told him all his troubles at once. How he wished to obey the King, and how his playmates had laughed at him, and how even his nurse and Christiana did not believe that the stories about the Celestial City were true.

Then Evangelist looked at him very kindly. "The stories are all quite true," he said. "The King loves little children. If you will obey Him and begin your journey, He will watch over you all the way, and when you reach the Celestial City you will be happy forever."

"I would go now," said little Christian, "if I only knew the way."

Evangelist turned round and looked across the field, along the path by which he had come. "Do you see there is a gate at the other side of the plain?" And he pointed to it with his finger.

But little Christian's eyes were still dim with tears, so that he could not see the gate.

"Well," said Evangelist, "there is a light shining above it. Can you see that?"

"Yes," said the little boy, "I think I can."

"The way to the Celestial City is through that gate. Now I will give you a message from the King," and Evangelist drew out a paper, which he put into little Christian's hand.

There were words written upon it in gold and beautiful colors, and Christian read them aloud—

> "I love them that love me,
> and those that seek me early
> shall find me."

"That is the King's promise to all His little children. So do not cry any more, but go quickly to that gate and knock. One of the King's servants will open it, and he will tell you where to go next."

3

Obstinate and Pliable

Some of the boys were playing near the gate of the city, and they saw Evangelist speaking to little Christian. They were not surprised at this, because they knew that the strangers from the Celestial City always talked to the children; but when Evangelist turned away, and little Christian began to run across the plain toward the Wicket-gate, they all wondered where he was going.

"Little Christian is running away!" cried one.

"He must be going to look for that Celestial City," said another.

"Then he will be lost!" exclaimed a third.

"We ought to go after him and bring him back."

There were two boys named Obstinate and Pliable, who knew little Christian very well. They were older than he was, but the three had often played together. Obstinate was not a pleasant companion, for he loved to have his own way, and Pliable used to give up to him for the sake of peace. Little Christian did not care much for either of them, but he liked Pliable best.

These two boys were vexed when they saw their little playmate running alone over the fields, for although they were often cross and disagreeable to him, they did not like to think of his being lost.

"We must make him come back," said Obstinate. "What a stupid boy he is to believe everything he is told!"

"Come along, then," said Pliable. "I will go with you."

So the two boys set off, and as they ran they shouted to little Christian to wait for them.

But the child was frightened when he heard their voices and would not even look round.

If they take me back, he thought, *perhaps I may never be able to get away again.*

He ran as fast as he could, but he soon began to feel tired because of the burden upon his back, and Obstinate and Pliable were taller and stronger than he was, so before long they overtook him.

"Where are you going?" cried Obstinate. "I wonder what you mean by making us run after you in this way!"

"I am going to the King's city," said little Christian. "Won't you come with me?"

Obstinate laughed. "I should think not! What would be the good, when we are as happy as possible at home?"

"We should be a great deal happier with the King. His city is more beautiful than this, and we shall be quite safe there. I have told you before that our own city is not a safe place."

"As if you knew anything about it!" said Obstinate. "Why do you talk such nonsense?"

"It is not nonsense. It is written in my Book."

Then Obstinate laughed again. "How many times am I to tell you that your Book is full of rubbish? There is not one word true. Now are you coming back or not?"

Obstinate looked very cross, and little Christian's heart began to beat faster and faster, but he answered bravely, "No, I am going to the King."

"Well, you may go, then," said Obstinate. "Come, Pliable, we might have saved ourselves the trouble of running after such a silly child. He doesn't know when he is well off."

But Pliable stood still. "Don't you laugh at him," he said. "Just supposing the Book *is* true, he will be better off than we are. I think I shall go too."

"Oh, do come with me!" cried little Christian. "You do not know how happy we shall be when we are living with the King."

"Are you sure you can find the city?" asked Pliable.

"Yes, for Evangelist told me what to do. We must go to that gate beyond the plain, and the man there will show us the way."

"You don't mean to say you are going?" said Obstinate. "Why, even if there were a Celestial City, two boys like you could never find it."

Pliable did not answer, but he made a few steps forward by the side of little Christian. He had often listened to the words of the strangers, and he thought, *I may as well go as far as the Wicket-gate and see what the road is like.*

"I'm not surprised at little Christian," continued Obstinate, "but really, Pliable, you ought to have more sense. Just come back with me, and I'll not tell anyone that you said you were going."

But Pliable was not very fond of Obstinate, and he felt pleased at the idea of having his own way; so he answered, "It's no use talking. I've made up my mind. Good-bye, if you won't come too.'"

"No, thank you; I'm glad enough to get rid of you both." And, with a mocking smile on his face, Obstinate turned back toward the City of Destruction.

4

The Slough of Despond

"Now," said Pliable, when the two boys were left alone, "tell me what sort of place this Celestial City is."

"It is very beautiful," replied little Christian. "Have you not heard the strangers talk about it? The King lives there, and His people never feel tired or unhappy. They wear shining clothes that can never be soiled and never grow old."

"I don't suppose they will let us in."

"Oh, yes, they will; Evangelist said so. See, he gave me this," and little Christian unfolded the King's message and let Pliable read the words for himself. "The King sent that to me, that I might know He would like me to go to His city."

"He hasn't sent me one."

"You didn't meet Evangelist. But never mind, I am *sure* the King will be pleased to see you."

"Well, tell me something else. What shall you do when you get to the city?"

"First of all I should like to see the King, and if He is very kind I shall ask Him where my mother is. You know she went away when I was a little baby, and sometimes I have wanted her so much. One of the strangers told me that she was with the King, so I think she must be living in the Celestial City."

"I wonder how long it will take us to get there. Did you ask Evangelist? We might walk a little faster, I think."

"I wish I could!" sighed little Christian, who was tired already. "I'm afraid I shall be a very long time on the way. It is this burden, which is so heavy that it makes me walk slowly."

Pliable was just going to say, "What do you mean by always pretending that you have a burden to carry?" when suddenly his feet sank deep into the grass, and he saw that he had walked into a marsh which lay in that part of the plain. "Oh!" cried he, "where are we now?"

"I don't know," said poor little Christian, whose burden made him sink deeper than Pliable into the soft green mud. "Let us try to get out."

But the boys were frightened and confused, and they could not tell which was the way out of the marsh. It was called the Slough of Despond, and it was a dangerous place even for grown-up people. Every step the children took seemed to lead them farther into it, and at last Pliable grew very angry.

"See what a mess we are in!" said he. "And it is all your fault! I wish I had not come. If this is the beginning of our journey, what else may we expect on the road? Just let me get out of this horrible marsh and I shall go straight home again. You may look for the city by yourself!"

Little Christian did not answer, for he was too frightened and unhappy to speak. His clothes were covered with mud, and every moment he feared that he would be smothered in the Slough. How he wished that Evangelist would come to help him, but he could not see anyone near to him. Far away, across the plain, shone the light above the Wicket-gate, and behind him lay the City of Destruction. Pliable turned away from the light, and at last succeeded in getting out of the marsh; but he never stopped to help his companion, and when little Christian looked back he saw him running home as fast as he could. Oh, how desolate the poor little boy felt when Pliable was out of sight!

"But I *will* go to the King!" he said, and once more he struggled on, trying to find some firm ground. Then, when he was almost in despair, he heard a voice saying, "Wait a bit, I am coming to help you."

5

Help Finds
Little Christian

*L*ittle Christian felt very much inclined to cry when he heard the voice of a friend. He had almost made up his mind that Evangelist was wrong, and that the King did not care to have little children traveling along the road to His beautiful city.

I am so small, he thought, *and so stupid! I cannot even get safely across this plain, and what should I do if I came to a high mountain or a deep river?*

But, just at that moment, a boy named Help, who was one of the King's servants, came near to the Slough and saw poor little Christian struggling in the mire. Help was a kind-hearted boy, and he ran at once to see what he could do for the child.

"How did you fall in?" he asked, but little Christian could not tell him.

"Evangelist said I was to go to the Wicket-gate, and I did not know about the marsh."

"Didn't you see the stepping stones?"

"No; I was talking to Pliable, and we were not looking at the ground."

"That was foolish. Where is Pliable?"

"He got out; but he went home and did not try to help me."

"Well, don't be frightened. I shall be able to reach you in a minute. The King will always take care of you. I wondered why He sent me over the plain today, but it was because He knew you would need me. Take hold of my hand, and put your foot here. There! You are quite safe."

Little Christian stood trembling, with tears in his eyes.

"You are very kind," he said. "I should never have got out by myself."

"No," replied Help, "I don't think you would. Are you going to the Celestial City?"

"I wish to go, but I am afraid the way will be too hard for me. Perhaps I had better wait until I am older."

"No, you must not wait. The King will watch over you, and whenever you need a friend to help you He will send somebody."

"Are you sure?" asked little Christian. "I am such a little boy, and the others all said I was stupid."

"Never mind what people say. If you are one of the King's pilgrims you are quite safe. You may find the road long and hard, but if you keep on bravely you will come to the city at last, and then you will forget your trouble, because you will be so glad to see the King."

Help spoke so kindly that little Christian did not feel afraid of talking to him.

"Do you think I shall find my mother in the Celestial City?" he said. "She is with the King."

"If she is with the King you will find her. Is it long since she went away?"

"She went when I was a little baby. I can't remember her at all, but we have her picture at home, so I shall be sure to know her. She looks so sweet and kind! Sometimes I cry because she cannot love me."

"But she *does* love you," said Help. "The King does not let His people forget. I have no doubt He has told her already that you are coming to the city, and she will be watching for you."

Help had been kneeling on the ground, wiping the mud from little Christian's clothes with tufts of soft grass. He rose now, saying, "You have soiled your things very much, but you will have new ones before you get to the city. Don't lose sight of the light over the Wicket-gate, and walk as quickly as you can until you reach it. Good-bye, and remember the King will take care of you."

"Just tell me one thing," said little Christian. "Have you been to the city yourself?"

"No. I have been very nearly to its gates, and then the King gave me some work to do for Him, and I shall not go to live in the city until it is finished."

"How long will it take me to get there?"

"I can't tell you that; for some people the journey is longer than for others. But if you love and obey the King, He will be sure to guide you to the city at the right time. Now I must go. If you are frightened again, cry to the King, and He will hear you."

6

Little Christian Meets with Worldly

Not very far from the City of Destruction there was a hill, and beyond the hill a little village. In this village lived a number of people who called themselves the King's servants and pretended to love and obey Him, although they did not really care about anything but their own pleasure and safety. They had been afraid to stay in the city, because of all that the strangers had told them, but they did not wish to have the trouble of going to the King's country; so they built houses and made fields and gardens for themselves beyond the hill, and fancied in that place they were quite safe.

A boy from the village, whose name was Worldly, happened to be walking across the plain on the very day little Christian began his journey. Worldly knew little Christian by sight, because the people from the village often went into the

city to visit their old friends; and when he saw the child coming he wondered what he was doing so far from home.

"Is that you, little Christian?" he said. "You are a long way from the city."

Worldly was a tall, fine-looking boy, and little Christian felt pleased to be noticed by him, so he answered at once, "I am going to the Wicket-gate."

"The Wicket-gate! What for?"

"To get rid of my burden."

"Oh, of course," replied Worldly. "I know those burdens are tiresome things. It isn't everybody who can feel them; but when you do feel them there is no comfort for you till they are gone."

Little Christian was surprised to hear Worldly speak in this way, for the boys and girls in the city had all laughed at him and had declared that his burden was only imaginary.

"I hope I shall not have to carry it very much longer," he said. "I am making haste to the Wicket-gate."

"Who put it into your head to go there?" asked Worldly.

"I met a very kind man, named Evangelist, and he told me to go."

Worldly laughed. "He may be very kind, but he is very stupid. I know him quite well. Look here, little Christian, I can tell you a much better way of losing your burden. Don't you trouble to go all that long journey. Yes, you see, I know exactly what Evangelist said to you. He tells everyone the same thing. You have been in that horrid slough already, and if you go through the Wicket-gate you will find worse troubles than that. There are wild beasts and all sorts of dangers, and very likely you will just die of hunger and fatigue."

"But my burden is *so* heavy," sighed little Christian. "I *must* get rid of it, and Evangelist said that was the best way."

"Well, of course you can do as you like," replied Worldly, "but I think you are very silly. How did you ever know that you had a burden at all?"

"I read in the King's Book that everyone has a burden."

"I thought so. That Book is all very well for clever, grown-up people, but little boys like you can't understand it.

You read it, and you don't know what it means, and you just get your head full of nonsense. Now, I'll tell you what to do. I wouldn't go back to the city, because you will always feel frightened, and it really isn't a very nice place to live in. If I were you, I should go round the hill to the village. I've some friends living in the first house you come to, and if you tell them that I sent you, they will take you in and be as kind as possible. Then in a few days you'll forget all about your burden, and I don't suppose you will ever feel it again."

Little Christian felt puzzled. Worldly spoke so kindly that he could scarcely help believing what he said, and he thought it would be very nice to live near to his old home and be able to see Christiana sometimes.

"You can't do better than take my advice," continued Worldly. "Never mind Evangelist. That is the way—past the hill. You can't mistake the house, because it is the first you come to."

Then he put his hands in his pockets and walked off whistling a merry tune; and little Christian forgot all about the King and His message, and turned away from the Wicket-gate to go to the village beyond the hill.

7

In the Wrong Path

*L*ittle Christian went on toward the village as quickly as he could, but he soon became very tired indeed. His burden seemed to grow heavier every minute, until at last he felt ready to fall down beneath its weight. By the time he reached the hill he could scarcely walk, and he wondered whether he would ever be able to get to the house in which the friends of Worldly lived.

But when he turned the corner of the road that led round the hill he almost forgot his burden, for he had never before seen anything so terrible as that path. The side of the hill was very rugged, and the rocks hung over the road and looked just ready to fall.

Christian went a little way, but he was soon so frightened that he dared not take another step. He fancied he could see flames of fire darting out between the rocks, and he shook all over with fear.

"Oh, I wish I had not come!" he sobbed. "What *shall* I do?"

Presently a man appeared at a little distance, and as he came nearer Christian saw that it was Evangelist. He had no smile on his face, and poor little Christian felt so ashamed and miserable that he almost wished the rocks *would* fall and hide him from the sight of the friend whom he had disobeyed.

"What are you doing here?" said Evangelist.

But little Christian hung down his head and did not speak.

"Are you not the little boy whom I found crying outside the City of Destruction?"

"Yes," sobbed Christian.

"Did I not show you the way to the Wicket-gate?"

"Yes."

"Then how is it you are here? For this is not the way to the gate."

"Oh," cried little Christian, "I did not mean to do wrong, but I met a boy who told me I could get rid of my burden in the village. And I was so tired I thought I would come; but I am sure the hill will fall on me, and I am *so* frightened!"

Then Evangelist said, "Listen to me. The King sent me to tell you about the Celestial City, and you had His promise that He would love you and watch over you. When you fell into the Slough, you know He sent Help to pull you out, and you have read in your Book that He will always take care of those who trust in Him. Why did you believe what Worldly said and turn away from the right path?"

Poor little Christian was now crying very bitterly, and Evangelist laid his hand gently on the child's head.

"You have grieved the King very much," he said, "but if you are sorry He will forgive you."

"I will never be naughty again," cried little Christian. "I am very, very sorry indeed. But are you sure that the King *will* forgive me?"

"Yes, the King will always forgive you, for the sake of His dear Son who loved the little children."

"And I may go back to the Wicket-gate, or will the man turn me away?"

"The King does not allow him to turn anyone away. You have only to knock, and he will open the gate for you at once. Take my hand, and I will go with you past the hill."

Little Christian wiped away his tears and was very glad to put his hand in Evangelist's and be led back into the fields. The hill, with its terrible overhanging rocks, was soon left behind, and the light above the Wicket-gate could be clearly seen.

"If you make haste," said Evangelist, "you will reach the gate before it is dark, and you can stay there and rest until morning."

Then, with a kiss and a smile, he told the child good-bye, and little Christian started once more on his journey.

8

Little Christian Enters the Wicket-Gate

The sun was just setting when little Christian reached the Wicket-gate. He had walked very quickly, for he did not wish to be in the fields after the darkness came on, and he was now so tired that he felt very glad indeed to see the gate quite close to him.

It stood in a beautiful stone archway, and over it hung a lamp, which burned so brightly that its light could be seen even when the sun was shining. Round the top of the arch some words were carved upon the stone, and little Christian stopped to read them. The words were these:

"KNOCK, AND IT SHALL BE OPENED UNTO YOU."

That was just what Evangelist said, thought Christian, and he began to knock upon the door. He listened, but he could not hear anyone coming, so he knocked again, and in a few minutes the door was opened by a man who looked something like Evangelist. He wore the same kind of long robe, and his face was grave and quiet. He smiled when he saw Christian, and said, "Who is this little child?"

"I am little Christian," replied the boy. "May I come in?"

"Are you come from the City of Destruction?" asked the man, whose name was Goodwill.

"Yes, and I wish to go to the King."

Then Goodwill opened the gate quite wide and took little Christian by the hand. As he was stepping in, Goodwill gave him a pull.

"Why did you do that?" asked Christian.

And Goodwill answered: "The Wicked Prince has a castle very near to this gate, and when he sees anyone leaving his country and entering the way of the King, he commands his soldiers to shoot arrows at him."

Little Christian looked out and saw the arrows lying upon the ground, and he felt very pleased to see Goodwill close the door.

"Now I am safe," he said.

Goodwill led him into his own house, which was just beyond the gate, and made him sit down to rest while he prepared some food for him.

"Who told you the way to the gate?" he asked.

"Evangelist," replied little Christian. "And he said you would tell me where to go next."

"Yes, I will tell you. But how is it that you came alone? Have you no father or mother?"

"My mother is with the King, and my father has so much to do that he cannot spare time for a journey, so I was obliged to come by myself."

"If your mother is with the King, she must have passed through this gate. No doubt you will hear of her as you go on your way."

"Do you think I shall?" said little Christian eagerly, for the greatest wish he had was to know something more of that dear mother whom he had lost so long ago. "Help said that the King would tell her I was coming, and she would look out for me. Is that true?"

"Quite true. You will not see her until you reach the Celestial City, but she will often be able to see you. Have you come straight from home? Did not the boys try to persuade you to stay with them?"

"Obstinate and Pliable came after me, and Obstinate was angry; but Pliable said he would like to go to the Celestial City. Then we fell into the Slough, and he was frightened, so he went back again. I thought I should never get out, but Help came, and he was very good to me."

"And what then?"

Little Christian blushed. "I was as bad as Pliable," he said, "for when I met Worldly, I listened to him and turned away toward the village. The road was so dreadful, and I was afraid the rocks would crush me. But Evangelist found me and brought me into the fields again."

"And now you have entered the King's gate, and you are one of His little pilgrims. Tonight you must sleep here, and tomorrow I will show you the way to the Celestial City."

9

Little Christian Visits the Interpreter

*W*hen the morning came, little Christian felt quite rested and ready for another day's journey. Goodwill brought him out and showed him a narrow pathway, which went straight across the plain.

"Are there any turnings?" asked Christian. "How shall I know if I come to a place where there are two roads?"

"The Way of the King is always quite straight," said Goodwill, "and all the paths that lead out of it are crooked. And the wrong paths are generally wide, while the right path is narrow. If you look carefully, you will not mistake it."

"I wonder whether you could unfasten my burden for me?" asked little Christian, when he was saying good-bye. "I could walk so much better without it."

"I cannot do that," said Goodwill. "You must carry it patiently until you come to the Cross, and then it will fall off, and you will never see it again."

"How glad I shall be!" sighed little Christian. "Are there any other houses on the way besides this one?"

"Yes, about the middle of the day you will pass the house of the Interpreter. He is very kind, and if you ask to see him he will show you many wonderful things."

The morning was bright and pleasant, and little Christian enjoyed his walk very much. The birds were singing so merrily that he felt as if he must sing with them, and the air was so fresh and sweet that it seemed to take away all the weariness that had troubled him in the City of Destruction.

There is nothing to hurt me here, he thought. *Worldly did not speak the truth when he said I should be frightened.*

Just when he was beginning to think that he would like to rest for a little while, he saw a large house standing near the road, and he knew that it must be the house of the Interpreter. He went up to the door and knocked, and presently a servant came to ask what he wanted.

"I am a little pilgrim," he said, "on my way to the King's city. I stayed at the Wicket-gate last night, and Goodwill told me that the master of this house is his friend. May I speak to him?"

The servant went back and called his master, and soon the Interpreter came out. He was an old man, with a tall figure and a long white beard, and Christian thought he looked very wise.

He put his hand on the child's head, saying, "What can I do for you, my little boy?"

"Would you mind showing me some of your wonderful things?" asked little Christian. He spoke timidly, for he could not help thinking that, although the Interpreter might be pleased to have grown-up visitors at his house, a little pilgrim like himself would perhaps be in the way. "Goodwill told me I might come to see you," he added.

The Interpreter smiled. "Goodwill is my friend," he said. "Are you one of the King's little pilgrims? Come in, and I will find something that you will like to see."

He took Christian's hand and led him into the hall, where the servant was still waiting. The Interpreter asked for a lamp, and when it was brought to him, he opened the door of a large room. Curtains were drawn before the windows, but the light of the lamp filled all the room with brightness. On the wall, opposite the door, hung a picture, and when little Christian saw it he clasped his hands and stood quite still.

It was the picture of a Man whose face was more beautiful than anything that little Christian had ever imagined. He was walking over a mountain path. All around Him, among the rocks, grew briars and thorns, which had torn His garments in many places, and His feet were bleeding, for the rough stones had wounded Him. In His arms He carried a little lamb. It was tired and had laid its head upon His shoulder, and He was looking down at it with gentle, loving eyes. Underneath the picture, in letters of gold, were written the words:

"HE SHALL GATHER THE LAMBS WITH HIS ARM,
AND CARRY THEM [NEAR HIS HEART"]

"Was the lamb lost?" asked little Christian.

"Yes," replied the Interpreter; "lost and ready to die. Do you not see how tired it looks, and how its fleece is torn and soiled? But the Good Shepherd heard its cry, and He never rested until He had found it, and then He brought it home in His arms."

"It must have been a hard path," said little Christian. "The stones have cut His feet."

"It was a very hard path, but He did not mind that, because He loved His little lamb. I have shown you this picture first, because the Good Shepherd is our King's own Son, and just as a shepherd loves his flock so He loves the pilgrims. The little pilgrims are like the lambs. You can think of this when you are sad or frightened, and remember who is watching over you."

"I am a little pilgrim," said Christian, looking up at the Interpreter.

"A little pilgrim, and a little lamb in the flock of the Good Shepherd. Now I will show you something else."

10

Passion and Patience, and the Brave Soldier

*L*ittle Christian felt quite sorry to turn away from the picture of the Good Shepherd. *I shall never forget it,* he thought. *The Shepherd's face is even more beautiful than my darling mother's.*

The Interpreter took him upstairs into a pleasant room, which looked like a nursery. Two little boys were sitting there, each in his own chair. One of them appeared to be quiet and happy, but the other was crying and seemed very cross and discontented.

"These two little boys are staying here for a time," said the Interpreter. "The one who is crying is called Passion, and his brother's name is Patience."

"Why is Passion crying?" asked Christian.

"He is a foolish boy," replied the Interpreter. "There are some beautiful gifts coming soon from the King, and the children are each to have their share. Patience is willing to wait for them, but Passion is vexed because he cannot enjoy them at once. He wishes to have his pleasure now, instead of at the proper time."

Just then the door opened, and a man came in, carrying a quantity of books and toys and pretty things, which he spread upon the table before Passion. The boy was delighted and, wiping away his tears, began to look at his treasures. Among them were some bags filled with bright golden coins, and when Passion saw these he held them up in his hands and laughed at Patience, who had nothing with which to amuse himself.

"Passion is very happy now," said the Interpreter, "but in a short time all his coins will be spent, and his pretty things will be torn and broken and spoiled, and when the King's gifts come he will have no share in them. Then he will wish he had waited as Patience is waiting."

"Are the King's gifts better than these?" asked little Christian.

"Far better. They are treasures that cannot be spoiled, and Patience is very wise to wait for them."

"Passion is laughing now," said Christian, "but I think Patience will have the best of it."

"I am sure he will," replied the Interpreter. "You must remember that everything I show you is meant to teach you something, and you may learn from this that it is not wise to wish too eagerly for pleasant things until the King sends them. He knows exactly what is good for each of us, and He will always give us what will make us really happy. If we behave like Passion and try to be happy in our own way, we are sure to be disappointed."

The Interpreter now took Christian out of the house and through his garden to a place from which they could see a beautiful palace, not very far off. The roof of the palace was flat, and upon it a number of people were walking about dressed in garments that shone brightly like gold.

"Is that one of the King's palaces?" asked little Christian.

"Yes, but it is not easy for anyone to enter it."

Outside the palace Christian saw a great crowd of men, who looked as if they wished to go in, but were afraid to do so. Then he saw that some other men, in armor, were standing round the doorway. They had fierce, cruel faces, and the men who were outside dared not try to pass by them. A little way from the door a man was sitting at a table, with a book before him, in which he wrote the name of anyone who tried to get into the palace.

Little Christian felt very much interested in all this, and he hoped that one of the men would be brave enough to go into the palace while he was there.

"Why does not the King drive away the wicked soldiers?" he said. "He *could* drive them away, and then all those people could go into the palace."

"He could do it quite easily," replied the Interpreter, "but He wishes to see how many of the people really care about entering the palace. Those who love the King with all their hearts are not afraid of the soldiers. We can wait for a little while, and you will see someone go in."

So they sat down upon the grass, and little Christian watched the people. Presently a man came out from the crowd and went toward the table near the doorway. His name was written in the book, and then he put on his helmet and drew his sword and rushed in among the soldiers. He fought with them for a long time, and Christian thought he would be killed; but although he received many wounds, he got into the palace at last, and then all the people upon the roof began to sing:

> "Come in, come in,
> Eternal glory thou shalt win."

Little Christian smiled. "Does that mean we are not to be frightened, because the King will help us and take us safely into His city?"

"Yes," said the Interpreter. "I thought you would understand it for yourself. Now, you have seen enough for one day. We must find a little bed for you, and tomorrow you shall go on your journey."

11

Little Christian Comes to the Cross

*L*ittle Christian slept very comfortably that night, and quite early in the morning he said good-bye to his kind friend.

Beyond the Interpreter's house the Way of the King was easy to find, for a high wall had been built on each side of the road. Little Christian thought this would make his journey less difficult, but the Interpreter told him that the wall did not go all the way to the Celestial City.

"When you have passed it," he said, "you must still keep to the straight path, and as long as you do that you will be safe."

Christian had almost forgotten his burden while he was with the Interpreter, but as he walked along and the day began to grow hot, he felt its weight again and wished that he could get rid of it.

Goodwill said I should lose it at the Cross, he thought. *I wonder if that is very far away.*

Presently he came to a place where there was a little hill by the side of the road, and upon the hill he saw the very thing for which he was longing. There stood the Cross, and the moment little Christian began to climb the path that led to it he felt that the bands which fastened his burden were breaking. Then it fell from his shoulders and rolled to the bottom of the hill, and when he turned to see what had become of it he found that it was quite gone.

At first he was so surprised that he could scarcely believe that he had really lost the burden that had been such a trouble to him.

I must be dreaming, he thought. But although he stood still for a few minutes, and rubbed his eyes, the burden did not come back. The birds went on singing, and the sun shone brightly upon the Cross, and he knew that he must be awake and that the King had really taken the weight from his shoulders forever.

"Now I can walk as quickly as I like," he said. And he stayed looking at the Cross, with his heart full of joy and thankfulness.

I told you before that the King's own Son had once come to visit the country in which little Christian lived; but, although He was kind and good to everyone, many of the people hated Him, and at last they seized Him and put Him to death in a very cruel manner, by nailing Him to a cross of wood. And this Cross was now placed by the wayside, that pilgrims to the Celestial City might see it and remember what had been done for their sakes. Little Christian had read of all this in his Book, and as he stood near the Cross he thought how very good the King's Son must be, and he did not wonder anymore why Evangelist and the other strangers loved Him so dearly and were never tired of talking about Him.

"Perhaps when they were pilgrims they carried burdens like mine," he said to himself. "And then, when they came to the Cross, they lost them, just as I have done. But I wish the people had not been so cruel to the King's Son!" And as he looked up at the Cross the tears came into his eyes.

Just then he heard a voice behind him saying, "Peace be to thee." Little Christian turned round quickly and saw three persons standing close to him. They wore shining white robes, and when Christian looked at them his eyes felt dazzled, as if he had been gazing at the sun.

They must have come from the Celestial City, he thought. *They are so bright and beautiful.*

"You have often displeased the King," said one of them, "but I have come to tell you that He has quite forgiven you, and the naughty things that you have done will not be remembered anymore."

Then the second took him by the hand, saying, "This little suit that you are wearing is torn and soiled. The King wishes His pilgrims to wear clothes that are clean and neat, so I have brought you some new ones."

And before little Christian had time to think what answer he should make, his shabby suit was taken off and he was dressed all in white.

Then the third set the King's mark upon his forehead and gave him a little roll of parchment in which, he said, Christian might read as he went along; and he must be sure to take care of it, for he would be asked to show it at the gate of the Celestial City.

After this the three Shining Ones went away, and little Christian was left to rejoice over all that the good King had done for him.

12

Simple, Sloth, and Presumption

You can fancy how very happy little Christian felt as he walked along.

"I have lost my burden," he said to himself, "and the King has given me these beautiful clothes! I think I would have started on my journey long ago if I had known how pleasant it is to be a little pilgrim."

Then he remembered Christiana, and he thought what a pity it was that she had not come with him. But he did not know how she would have managed it, for she had three brothers, besides her baby sister, and she had to take care of them all.

We might have taken turns carrying the baby, he thought. *But even then the boys would have been very tired. Perhaps when I get to the City I might ask the King to send someone to help her with the children, for I should like her to come too.*

Then he wondered whether his mother had told the King that she had left a little boy behind her in the City of Destruction, and whether she would know that his burden had been taken away and that the King had sent him such beautiful gifts.

They are so very beautiful, he thought, as he looked down once more at the clothes in which the Shining One had dressed him. *They are as white as snow, and they are not the least bit hot and heavy, as my old ones were.*

He was walking on with his mind full of these things when he saw, just before him, three boys lying on the grass by the side of the road. He stopped to look at them as he passed, and then he found that they were all fast asleep and that their feet were bound together with bands of iron.

The day was very hot, and these boys had foolishly turned out of the path and had lain down to rest for a little while. The servants of the Wicked Prince were always on the watch for careless pilgrims, and as soon as the lads were asleep they had hastened to bind their feet, so that, unless the King Himself sent someone to help them, they would never be able to take another step toward the Celestial City.

Little Christian felt that it would be unkind to leave them lying there, so he went up to them and called to them.

"You had better get up," he said. "This is not at all a safe place to sleep in. Don't you know that someone has bound your feet together?"

Then one of them, whose name was Simple, answered, without even opening his eyes, "What is the matter? I don't see anything to hurt. Do let one have a minute's peace!"

But little Christian said, "I am sure you are in great danger. Make haste, and let me help you to undo these irons."

The boy who lay next to Simple was named Sloth, and at last he sat up and began to rub his eyes in a very sleepy way. He looked at little Christian, but he would not listen to his advice.

"What is the use of disturbing us?" he said. "Just go on. I shall be coming soon, when I have had a good rest."

And the third boy, who was called Presumption, said, "Surely we can do as we like! If we choose to sleep in a dangerous place it is our business, not yours. So go on your journey, and don't meddle with other people."

Then they both lay down again by the side of Simple, and in a few minutes Christian saw that they were all sleeping as soundly as before. It was of no use for him to waste his time over such idle, foolish boys, so he was obliged to turn away, feeling very sorry that they would not listen to him or believe that they were in the power of the Wicked Prince.

13

Formalist and Hypocrisy

*W*hen little Christian had gone some distance from the place where the three boys lay sleeping, he turned and looked back, thinking that perhaps they might now be fully awake and more anxious to be freed from their iron fetters. But he could not see anything of them, and he was just moving on again when he heard a noise on his left hand and saw two boys climbing upon the wall. They both dropped over into the Way of the King, and seeing little Christian they ran up to him.

"Where have you come from?" he asked.

The boys, whose names were Formalist and Hypocrisy, answered, "We have been living in the land of Vainglory, but we are now going to the Celestial City to see the King."

"But don't you know," said little Christian, "that you should have come in at the Wicket-gate?"

"Oh," cried the boys, "that is much too far from our country! We just made a short cut across the fields and came over the wall."

Little Christian thought that the King would not like people to begin their pilgrimage in this way, and he said, "I am afraid you ought not to have done so."

"Oh, don't you bother about it," said they. "Our people never go round by the gate. Besides, what does it matter, so long as we get onto the right road? You came in by the Gate, and we came over the wall, and now we are all exactly in the same place."

"I don't think you ought to have done it," said little Christian.

"What nonsense!" they replied. "We are just as good pilgrims as you are, except that you have such fine clothes, which very likely somebody had to give you because your own were not fit to be seen."

This was a very rude and unkind speech, and little Christian felt inclined to answer back in the same way. But he had read in his Book that the King's servants ought always to speak gently, even when angry words were spoken to them, so he waited a minute and then said quietly, "That is quite true. My things were all spoiled and shabby, and the King gave me these clothes Himself. It was very kind of Him, and I am very glad He did it, because now I am sure that, when I get to the City, He will know that I am one of His own little pilgrims. And the Shining One has set the King's mark on my forehead, and I have a Roll which I am to show at the end of my journey. You have not any of these things, because you did not come in at the Wicket-gate."

But the boys only laughed, so little Christian left them and walked on by himself.

Presently they all came to the foot of the hill called Difficulty. The Way of the King led over the hill. It was very rough and very steep, but little Christian knew that he must not turn away from it. A spring of cool water was flowing just by the wayside, so, as he was very thirsty, he took a refreshing drink and then began to climb the rocky path.

Formalist and Hypocrisy were a little way behind Christian, and when they came to the hill they saw two paths, which turned one to the right and the other to the left out of the straight road.

"What is the good of climbing up that steep place?" they said. "These two paths are smooth and easy, and as they go round the hill they must come into the King's Way again on the other side."

So Formalist said, "I will go along this path," and Hypocrisy said, "I will go along that one," and the boys parted, believing that they would meet again very soon.

Now, if they had entered by the Wicket-gate, they would have known, as little Christian did, that the straight road was the only safe one; but I am sorry to tell you that both these foolish boys were lost, because they had not taken the trouble to obey the King and begin their pilgrimage in the right way.

Formalist had entered the path of Danger, and very soon he found himself in a great wood. He wandered about for many nights and days, but he could not find his way out of it, and so at last he died of hunger and cold.

The path of Destruction, which Hypocrisy had chosen, was no better. It led into the midst of some dark mountains, where the boy went up and down until his foot slipped and he fell, wounding himself upon the sharp rocks, so that he too perished miserably.

14

The Hill Difficulty

*L*ittle Christian found the path up the hillside a very hard one. It was covered with rough stones and sharp pieces of rock, which hurt his feet, and it became steeper and steeper as he went on, until at last he was obliged to creep along on his hands and knees. The sun was now shining very brightly, for it was the middle of the day, and its rays fell upon little Christian and made him feel hot and tired.

What should *I have done*, he thought, *if I had had to climb this hill yesterday? I could never have carried my burden up such a dreadful road!*

When he was about halfway up the hill the path became easier. He was able to walk again, and the stones did not seem to be quite so sharp. Still, it was hard work climbing, and when he came presently to a little shady arbor he was very glad indeed. This arbor had been built by order of the King, so that His pilgrims might have a place in which to rest on their way over the hill.

Little Christian went in and sat down. It was cool and quiet, and he thought he would now have time to look at the Roll that the Shining One had given to him. So he took it out and read in it for a little while. Then, instead of making haste to the top of the hill, he sat idly in the arbor, looking at his new clothes and thinking of many things, until his eyes closed and he fell asleep.

He did not wake until late in the afternoon, and when he looked at the sky and saw that it was already beginning to grow crimson with the sunset, he started up and began to walk as quickly as he could.

Before he reached the top of the hill he met two boys running very fast indeed. Their faces were white with fear, and their whole bodies were trembling, but when they saw little Christian they stopped to speak to him.

"What is the matter?" he asked. "You are running the wrong way."

"Oh," cried the eldest, whose name was Timorous, "we were going to the City of the King, and we had climbed up this terrible hill, but the farther we go the more danger we find, so we are hurrying home again."

"Yes," said the other, who was called Mistrust, "there are two great lions lying just in the way, and we don't know whether they are asleep or not. But I am sure if we try to pass them we shall be torn to pieces."

Then little Christian began to feel frightened too, and he said, "What shall I do?"

"Why, come back with us," said Timorous. "You cannot be so foolish as to venture near those savage beasts!"

"I don't know," replied little Christian. "If I go back I shall never see the King."

"Well, you will not see Him if you go on," said Mistrust, "for the lions will kill you."

But little Christian remembered that Evangelist and Goodwill and the kind Interpreter had all told him that, although he might often be frightened and in trouble, the King would surely help him and take care of him.

"I don't think I will turn back," he said. "The lions may not be awake. Let us all go together."

"Oh, no!" cried Timorous and Mistrust. "We dare not. We shall just make the best of our way home again—and be very thankful when we get there safely."

So they ran down the hill and left little Christian to go on his way alone.

He could not help being frightened, and he thought, *I will look at my Roll and see whether there is anything written in it about these lions.*

But when he put his hand into the breast of his jacket the Roll was not there, and though he felt carefully among his clothes, he could not find it anywhere.

"Where *can* it be?" he said, and he stood still to think how he could possibly have lost it. He was in very great trouble, for he remembered that the Shining One had told him to take care of the Roll, for he would be asked to show it at the gate of the Celestial City.

"I cannot go without it," he cried. "Oh, what shall I do?" And the tears began to roll down his cheeks.

15

Little Christian Comes to the Palace Beautiful

*T*he loss of his Roll made poor little Christian very miserable. He forgot all about the lions in his trouble and could think only of his carelessness in losing the most precious of the King's gifts. Suddenly he remembered the shady arbor in which he had spent the afternoon. Perhaps the Roll might have fallen there, and when he started up so hurriedly he might not have seen it.

"Oh, how could I be so foolish?" he cried. "I ought only to have rested there, and I wasted so much time, and now it will be night before I reach the top of the hill."

He turned round and went back slowly, looking carefully at the path lest he might have dropped the Roll on his way. At last he reached the arbor, and there, upon the floor, just under the bench upon which he had been sitting, he saw his lost treasure.

We may fancy how eagerly he caught it up and how thankful he felt to the King for letting him find it again.

But this search for the Roll had hindered the little pilgrim, and although he climbed the steep path once more as quickly as he could, the sun had gone out of sight before he reached the top of the hill, and the light was fading very fast.

It is all my own fault, he thought. *If I had not been so idle I should not have lost my Roll, and I might have had time to find a place to rest in before the night.*

Then he remembered the lions, and he wondered how far he was from the spot where they lay. He knew that these savage beasts always prowl about in search of their prey during the darkness, and as the shadows grew deeper and deeper round him he felt more and more afraid.

Just when the light had become very dim indeed a large building appeared in the distance, and as Christian hurried along he saw that it was a great palace and that the Way of the King would lead him close to its gates. A little cottage stood within the gates, which he supposed must be the doorkeeper's lodge, and he walked quickly toward it, hoping that he might be allowed to stay there for the night.

The path now became very narrow indeed, and when he had almost reached the palace gates Christian saw the two lions, which had so frightened Mistrust and Timorous, lying just before him, one on each side of the way. The lions were chained, but it was too dark for the chains to be seen, and little Christian stood still, wondering what he should do. There was only a very small space between the lions, and he thought that if he ventured to pass them they would surely spring upon him.

The name of the doorkeeper was Watchful, and he knew how much the pilgrims feared the lions, so he came very often to the door of his house to see if anyone was coming near. When he saw little Christian he called to him, saying, "Don't be frightened; the lions are both chained. Keep in the middle of the path, and they will not hurt you."

So Christian went on, trembling and very much afraid, but he was careful to keep in the middle of the path, and although the great creatures roared as he walked between them, they lay still and did not even stretch out their huge paws to touch him.

When he had passed the lions little Christian clapped his hands for joy and ran quickly toward the kind doorkeeper, who stood at the gates.

"What palace is this?" he asked.

"It is called the Palace Beautiful," said Watchful, "and it belongs to the King. He built it for His pilgrims to use. Are you going to the Celestial City?"

"Yes," answered little Christian. "I slept last night at the house of the Interpreter. Do you think I may stay here until the morning?"

"How is it that you are traveling so late?" asked the porter.

Then little Christian had to tell of his idleness in the afternoon, and how he had lost his Roll and had been obliged to go back to look for it.

"Well," said Watchful, "I will call the lady of the house, and if you are one of the King's little pilgrims she will take care of you."

So they went together to the door of the palace, and the doorkeeper rang the bell.

16

New Friends

*L*ittle Christian waited by the side of Watchful in the porch of the Palace Beautiful, and presently a lady came out to speak to them. Her name was Discretion, and when Christian looked up at her he thought her face was the sweetest he had ever seen.

"Why did you call me?" she asked. Then, seeing little Christian, she put out her hand and laid it gently on his shoulder.

She is like my mother's picture, he thought. *I am sure I shall love her.*

Watchful answered his mistress, saying, "This boy is journeying to the Celestial City, and it is too late for him to walk any farther tonight, so he would be glad to stay here if you are willing to take him in."

Then Discretion asked little Christian many questions. She wished to know from what city he had come, and why he had left his home. She also asked him who had directed him into the way of the King, and she made him tell her of all that had happened to him on his journey.

"And what is your name?" she said at last.

"Christian," he replied. "I shall be so very glad if I may stay here until the morning."

"Yes, you may stay," answered Discretion, smiling at the boy's anxious little face. "Wait, and I will call my daughters."

She went back into the house and brought out three girls. Two of them were older than Christian. Their names were Piety and Prudence. Charity, the youngest, was just about his own age. "This is one of the King's little pilgrims,"

said Discretion. "I think we can make room for him in the palace, can we not?"

"Oh, yes!" said Prudence, and Charity ran up to him and put her hand in his, as Christiana used to do when he was at home.

"Come in," said Piety. "We are very glad to see you."

A number of people were in the hall of the palace, and they all looked kindly at little Christian as he came in.

"Mother takes care of them," said Charity. "We girls look after the little pilgrims."

"It is not quite time for supper," said Discretion, "but no doubt Christian is tired. Take him into your own room and let him rest."

The three girls led the way to a comfortable room, where a lamp was burning and casting its cheerful light upon walls that were covered with beautiful pictures. Here Christian sat down, while Piety and Prudence took up the needlework that they had laid aside when their mother called for them. Charity brought a footstool and seated herself near to Christian. She was a kindhearted little girl and loved to spend her time in waiting upon her mother's guests and in doing all she could to make them happy.

"If you are not too tired to talk," said Piety, "we should like to hear about your journey. What made you leave your home?"

"I was frightened," answered Christian, "for the strangers who came to our city used to tell us that it would be destroyed."

"And how was it that you thought of coming into the Way of the King?"

"I had read of the Celestial City in my Book, and one day Evangelist met me, and he showed me the way to the Wicket-gate."

"Did you stay at the house of the Interpreter?"

"Oh, yes," replied Christian. "He was very kind to me. I saw the picture of the Good Shepherd, and I watched the soldier who fought his way into the palace. I wish I could have stayed there a long time!"

"And what have you done today?"

"First, I passed by the Cross, and there I lost my burden, and the Shining Ones brought me these new white clothes. They gave me a message from the King, and one of them set this mark upon my forehead. After that I found three boys sleeping by the wayside. I tried to wake them, but they would not listen to me. Then Formalist and Hypocrisy climbed over the wall, but I think they chose the wrong path when we came to the hill, for I did not see them again."

"The hill is hard to climb," said Piety.

"Yes, I thought I should never get up. And then, when I saw the lions, I very nearly turned back again, but the keeper called to me and told me they were chained."

Then Prudence began to question the little pilgrim.

"Do you ever think about your old home?" she asked.

"Yes," said Christian. "I often think about it."

"Have you sometimes wished to go back again?"

"Once or twice, when I have been very tired. But I am sure the Celestial City is far better than ours, and I know I shall be happy when I get there."

"Why shall you be happy?"

"I shall see the Prince,' said little Christian. "It was so cruel of the wicked people to nail Him to the Cross, and I love Him because He died for our sakes. Then my mother is with the King. She went away when I was a baby, but I shall know her because I have seen her picture."

"Have you any little sisters?" asked Charity.

"No, but Christiana used to play with me. She is kind and gentle."

"Why didn't you bring her with you?" said Charity. "Then you would have had someone to talk to on the way."

"She did not believe what the strangers said," replied Christian. "And she has her brothers to take care of. They have no father or mother, and Christiana has to do everything herself."

"Didn't you talk to her and beg her to come with you?"

"I often told her about the City, but, you know, I might not have come myself if Evangelist had not shown me the way. And then I started at once, so that I didn't even say good-bye to Christiana."

"Well, perhaps Evangelist will find her, and then she will come and bring her brothers with her."

Just at this moment a bell rang, and the two older girls folded up their work, saying, "This is to tell us that our supper is ready."

Little Christian was hungry as well as tired, and he enjoyed the good food that was set before him. Then Discretion herself took him upstairs into a pleasant room with a window looking toward the east, and there the weary little pilgrim slept soundly until he was awakened by the light of the rising sun.

17

A Happy Day

*W*hen the morning came little Christian supposed that he would have to continue his journey, but as soon as breakfast was over he heard the gentle voice of Discretion desiring him to come to her.

"I think it will do you good to stay with us for a few days," she said. "You have walked a long way since you left home, and it is not well for little pilgrims to travel too quickly at first."

"I should like to stay," said Christian, "if I shall not be in the way."

"You will not be in the way at all. Taking care of little pilgrims is part of the work that my daughters have to do for the King, and we are always glad to have children staying at the palace."

"Did my mother stay here? Her name was Peace, and I think she must have come this way when the King sent for her. It is a long time ago. I was quite a little baby when she went away."

"We will look in the records for her name. If she stayed here, it will be written down."

"I think she was a little, just a *little* bit like you," said Christian, timidly.

Discretion bent down and kissed the child, for she saw the tears in his eyes.

"You will find her again, little Christian," she whispered. "And do you know that she is often very near to you? You cannot see her, but she can see you. The King is very good, and He knows how mothers love their little ones."

"I shall see her in the King's City?"

56

"Yes, and then you will never lose her again."

"And my father?" said little Christian, anxiously. "Will he *always* be busy, or do you think he will someday be able to come too?"

"I cannot tell," replied Discretion. "I am sure the King will not leave off sending messages to him, and perhaps when he knows that you and your mother are so happy he will wish to be with you, and he will begin his pilgrimage."

"He will not be frightened on the way," said Christian, "because he is a man, and very brave. I think, perhaps, even Mother did not like passing the lions. When my father comes, will you tell him that I stayed here and that when he gets to the gates of the Celestial City he will be sure to see me watching for him?"

"Yes, I will tell him," answered Discretion. "Now, I have many things to do, so Charity shall take you into the library, and you may look in the records for your mother's name."

Christian spent a very happy day at the palace. Sometimes Charity was with him, and sometimes Prudence, and sometimes Piety, but they were all kind and gentle and did everything they could to please their little guest.

Christian, like many other boys, loved to read stories and to look at pictures, and he found much to enjoy in the library of the Palace Beautiful. Prudence told him which books to read, and Piety showed him all the pictures. There were many pictures of children: like Moses lying in his cradle of rushes by the waterside; little Samuel lighting the lamps in the House of God; and little Timothy listening to his mother's teaching.

"And this is our dear Prince Himself," said Piety. "You have read in your Book how He came down to live among us and was a little baby in a poor home. Here you see Him in the arms of His mother, and the shepherds are kneeling round Him."

Christian liked this picture and stood before it for some time, until Charity called him to look at one that was her favorite. It was called "The Guardian Angel." A little child was walking along a very narrow path, and close behind him came a beautiful angel, with her hands spread out to touch his shoulders on either side.

"You see, he cannot fall," said Charity. "The King has sent the angel, and if he slips she will hold him fast."

The time passed so quickly that the little pilgrim was surprised when evening came. Discretion had been busy all day, but before the lamps were lighted she came into the library where Christian was reading. He laid down his book, and she drew him into her arms and talked to him in a low, gentle tone, telling him many things about their good King and the Prince, His Son.

"I have never spent such a happy day in all my life," said Christian when he went to bed. "If it were not that I wish so much to live in the King's City, I should like to stay here always."

18

Little Christian Receives His Armor

*L*ittle Christian spent three whole days at the Palace Beautiful. On the second day Discretion allowed him to see the armory. This was a large room in which were stored all kinds of weapons for the use of the king's servants.

Here Christian saw long rows of shining helmets, shields, and breastplates of the finest brass, glittering swords, and shoes that Charity told him could never be worn out. And he noticed that these things were not all intended for grown-up persons. There were helmets that he felt sure were too small even for him, and tiny swords that seemed only fit for children to play with.

"Are they toys?" he asked.

"No," said Piety, "they are for the little pilgrims."

Then Christian could not help thinking how very much he would like to have a sword and shield of his own, and be one of the King's little soldiers.

Piety sat down by one of the windows in the armory and told Christian about the wonderful things that some of the King's soldiers had done. The story he liked best was that of a boy named David, who, when he was young, had fought with a great giant and had been able to kill him.

"The giant was one of the King's enemies," said Piety, "and he thought he could easily kill little David. He was covered with armor from head to foot, and David wore only a shepherd's dress and carried neither sword nor spear."

"What did he fight with?" asked Christian.

"He had a sling and a stone, and when he threw the stone at the giant the King helped him, and he aimed so well that he struck the giant on the forehead and killed him."

This story comforted little Christian, for if the King had helped David, no doubt He would be ready to help any other little pilgrim who trusted in Him.

On the third day Christian said to Prudence, "Is it not time for me to go on my journey?"

"Not yet," answered Prudence. "It is misty this morning, and you have not seen the view from the roof of the palace."

So little Christian spent another happy day.

In the morning, when he opened his window, he found that the mist had all passed away, and as soon as breakfast was over the three girls took him up to the roof. It was flat, so that people could easily walk upon it or even sit there in the pleasant summer weather.

Christian looked toward the south, and, far away in the distance, he could see a long range of beautiful hills, with broad green fields and vineyards and shady woods. He could even see the streams sparkling in the sunlight as they flowed down into the quiet valleys.

"Oh," he exclaimed, "what a lovely country that must be!"

"Yes," said Piety. "That is Immanuel's Land, and the Way of the King passes through it. The hills are called the Delectable Mountains, and from them you will be able to see the gates of the Celestial City."

"Will it take me long to get there?" asked Christian.

"I do not know," answered Piety. "You are a little pilgrim, and you cannot travel very fast."

Just then they heard the voice of Discretion calling to them.

"We must let little Christian start in good time," she said, "in order to reach the valley before the sun is hot."

"I am ready," began Christian, but Charity interrupted him.

"No, he is not ready—is he, Mother? We have something more to do for him, have we not?"

"Yes," replied Discretion, and she led the way to the armory. "Between the palace and the Celestial City the King's enemies are often very troublesome, and even the little pilgrims need to carry weapons."

Christian's cheeks glowed with pleasure when he found that he was really to have a suit of armor for his very own, and Discretion and her daughters seemed pleased also.

"I like to see you made into a soldier," said Charity, and Christian wished that Christiana could have been there too.

"You must take care of your armor," said Discretion, as she chose out a helmet of the right size. "It must always be kept bright and shining."

Then Piety brought him a shield, which was just large enough to protect him and not too heavy for him to carry.

Prudence fastened the sword at his side, and Charity fitted on his shoes, and then, when he was completely dressed, Discretion bent down and kissed him as she had done before, saying, "May the blessing of the King go with you, my child, and may you continue His faithful soldier and servant all the days of your life!"

Little Christian felt too happy to speak, so he just put his arms around Discretion as if she had been his own mother, and she well understood that his heart was full of love and gratitude. "You must thank the King," she said. "It is He who gives you all these things."

19

An Enemy

Watchful was standing at the door of the lodge when little Christian came out of the palace. When he was opening the gates he told Christian that another boy-pilgrim had passed by.

"I asked him his name," said the porter, "and he told me it was Faithful."

"Oh," cried little Christian, "I know him very well! His house was quite near to ours. How long has he been gone? Do you think I can overtake him?"

"It is about half an hour since I saw him," replied Watchful. "I should think by this time he will be at the bottom of the hill."

Christian was so pleased at the thought of having a companion that he determined to walk as quickly as possible, in order to overtake Faithful. But first he must say goodbye to his kind friends, who had all come down to the gates with him.

"It is a beautiful morning," said Discretion. "Suppose we go to the foot of the hill with little Christian?"

"That would be very nice," said Charity, "and perhaps we may find Faithful there. I wonder why he did not come in to.see us?"

"It is early," said Discretion, "and no doubt he wished to hasten on his journey."

I told you that the Palace Beautiful was built at the top of the Hill Difficulty. The valley below was called the Valley of Humiliation, and the path that led down into it from the gates of the palace was very steep indeed. Christian was glad when Discretion took his hand and held it tightly in her own, for he could scarcely keep from slipping.

"I think it is difficult to get up this hill—and dangerous to go down," he said.

"Yes," replied Prudence, "people sometimes have bad falls upon this path."

It was not long before they found themselves in the valley, and then Discretion gave Christian a little package of food, which she had brought with her.

"We have been very glad to see you," she said, "and I shall not forget to give your message to your father when he comes to the palace."

Little Christian was quite sorry to say good-bye, and when Discretion and her daughters had left him he felt very lonely indeed. The valley was quiet and cool, and he walked on quickly, hoping soon to see Faithful in the distance before him. But instead of Faithful, he presently saw a very evil-looking man coming along the path to meet him. The man was tall and strong, and his face was not a pleasant one. As he drew near Christian remembered his name, for he had seen him before. He was one of the chief officers in the army of the Wicked Prince, and he was called Self.

He is one of the King's Enemies, thought Christian, *and he will try to hurt me. What shall I do?*

At first he thought he would turn around and run toward the foot of the hill. Discretion might look back and see him, or, perhaps, Watchful might be at the palace gates and would send someone to help him. But then he remembered that he had no armor for his back and that his breastplate and shield would be of no use to him unless he faced his enemy. So he determined to trust in the King and go straight on. Perhaps, as he was such a little boy, Self would pass by without taking any notice of him. He walked on steadily, and in a few minutes Self was quite close to him.

"I should like to know where you have come from," he said, stopping in front of Christian and looking down at his bright armor.

Christian felt very much frightened, but he answered, "From the City of Destruction."

"And where are you going?"

"To the City of the King."

"Perhaps you have forgotten," said Self, "that the City of Destruction belongs to me. If you were not a little boy, who can be taken back again, I should kill you for running away without my leave."

"I know the city belongs to you," replied Christian bravely, "but the King loves me better than you do, and I would rather live with Him."

Then Self smiled.

"Don't be foolish!" he said. "I can be very kind to people when I like them, and if you will come back with me, and promise not to run away again, I will not be angry with you. You shall live in my house and be one of my own servants."

"I am one of the King's servants," said Christian.

"That does not matter. The King's servants often run away from Him. Besides, you were *my* servant when you were at home, and you ought to be very glad that I am willing to forgive you and take you back again."

Poor little Christian felt that tears were coming into his eyes, and his lips were beginning to tremble, but he answered, "I love the King, and I would rather be His servant. Please let me go on."

But Self had made up his mind that Christian should go home with him, so he said, "Don't be in a hurry! Just think of all the trouble you may meet with on the way. Our soldiers are up and down everywhere, and if they see you, and try to hurt you, I don't suppose the King will take the trouble to help a child. You know you have served Him very badly since you set out. You were so careless that you fell into the Slough, and you let Worldly deceive you and turn you out of the right path. Then you slept in the arbor and lost your Roll, and when you came in sight of the lions you were very nearly turning back for fear of them. And yet, at the Palace Beautiful, you talked as if you were one of the King's most faithful servants! I don't know how you can expect Him to do anything for you."

Little Christian knew that all these things were true, and he wondered how Self had heard about them.

"I have been very sorry," he said, "and the King will forgive me. He knows I am only a little boy."

Then Self could not keep back his anger any longer. He had been speaking gently, because he wished Christian to forsake the King of his own accord, but when he saw that his words were of no use he became fierce with passion.

"I hate your King," he cried, "and everybody and everything belonging to Him! You are my servant, and you shall never go to the Celestial City, for I will kill you."

20

The First Battle

*L*ittle Christian had scarcely time to put up his shield before Self began to throw fiery darts at him, and he feared that he would soon be killed by them. But the story he had heard at the Palace Beautiful of David and the giant came into his mind, and he thought, *David had only his shepherd's dress, and I am wearing the good armor that the King has given me. I will trust in Him and try not to be afraid.*

So he held his shield firmly on his arm and caught nearly all Self's darts upon it, until the wicked soldier became wild with rage, and rushing suddenly at little Christian he seized him in his strong arms. Those darts which Christian had not been able to catch upon his shield had struck him and wounded him in his hands and feet. His wounds were very sore and were bleeding so much that he was beginning to feel faint. Self had seen this, and he flung the child upon the ground, thinking he would now be able to kill him. Little Christian had drawn out his sword from its sheath, but when

Self threw him down, it fell from his hand, and as he lay on the path he thought he had now no chance of escaping from his cruel enemy. But just as Self was going to strike his last blow, Christian saw that the sword lay within his reach. He put out his hand and caught it up, and before Self had time to prevent him, he thrust it into the soldier's body and gave him a terrible wound.

Now the soldiers of the Wicked Prince could not bear the pain of a wound given with one of the King's swords, and Self cried out when Christian struck him. Then the boy's courage came back to him, and he thrust the weapon at his enemy a second time, and after that Self fled away across the valley, and Christian was left alone.

He lay for a minute upon the path, and then he got up and looked around. All over the grass lay the sharp darts that had been thrown at him, but Self was gone. Christian could not see him anywhere.

It was the King who helped me, he thought, and his heart was full of thankfulness for his wonderful deliverance.

But the poor little soldier had been sadly wounded, and he felt so faint and ill that he was obliged to sit down upon the grass and lean his head against a great rock. He was weak and tired, and I think he must have fallen asleep, for he had a strange dream.

He thought that his mother came across the valley—his own darling mother, whom he had lost so long ago. Her face shone, as little Christian had seen the moonbeams shining on a dark night. A soft, silvery light seemed all around her. She was more beautiful than Discretion, and her eyes, as she looked at him, were full of love and pity. Little Christian stretched out his hands to her, and she came toward him and knelt down on the grass and took him in her arms. Then she tenderly dressed the wounds, and he lay quite still and wondered if she were an angel. She did not speak to him, but presently she laid him down again upon the grass, and then he felt her lips touch his forehead.

"Mother! Mother!" he cried, and he opened his eyes, but she was not there. He was lying by the rock, and he could see all down the long valley. He was quite alone. He sat up and looked at his wounds. They were not bleeding now, and they did not even ache.

I must have been dreaming, he thought. *And yet the wounds are all healed! Perhaps it was my mother. They said she would often be near to me. Oh, I think the King might have sent her to help me, when He saw I was sick and faint. Or at least He must have sent one of His Shining Ones!*

Then he remembered that Discretion had given him some food, so he sat still for a little while and ate the bread and meat that she had given him.

I must make haste, he thought, *for I have lost so much time. I wonder whether Self has really gone quite away, or whether he will come back to look for me again. And he said the soldiers were all around. I must be ready to meet them.*

So he kept his sword in his hand and looked carefully from side to side, among the rocks and bushes, as he went along.

21

The Dark Valley

*I*t was late in the afternoon when little Christian came to the end of the Valley of Humiliation. He had seen nothing more of his enemy Self, and he was beginning to think that he might now put his sword back into its sheath, when he saw two boys running toward him. Their faces were white, as those of Mistrust and Timorous had been, and as they came up to him Christian said to them, "Where are you going?"

"Back! Back!" cried the boys. "If you care for your life you had better come with us."

"Why?" asked Christian. "What is the matter?"

"Matter!" they answered. "We were going to the Celestial City, as you are, but we have been as far as we dare. Indeed, if we had ventured a few steps farther, we should never have had the chance to come back and save you."

"What did you find?" said Christian, wondering what dangers he might have to pass through that night. He had no thought of turning back, for his victory over Self had made him love and trust his good King more than ever; but he wished to know what the boys had seen, so that he might be prepared to defend himself.

"Just before us," they said, "is the Dark Valley, but we saw it in time, and we have hurried away."

"What is it like?"

"It is terrible! It is the most dreadful place we have ever seen, full of darkness, and we could hear cries and groans of people in pain. No doubt they are pilgrims who have been lost there."

"The Way of the King leads straight through it," said Christian.

"Yes," replied the boys.

"Then I do not see how we are to escape it."

"*You* can try it if you like," said they, "but if we get to that city at all it must be by some other road than that."

So they left him, and little Christian went on, keeping his sword in his hand.

The Dark Valley lay much lower than the Valley of Humiliation. It was narrow, and the black rocks seemed almost to meet over Christian's head as he entered it. The evening was coming on, and the path was soon surrounded with a thick mist, so that he could scarcely see his hand when he stretched it out before him. Flashes of light kept breaking through the mist, but he did not know whether they were flames of fire or lightning, and the air was filled with terrible sounds, which made his heart beat fast with fear. By the light of the flames he saw that the path upon which he was walking was a very dangerous one. On his right hand there was a very deep hollow, and on his left a marsh, and it was all he could do to prevent himself from slipping into either one or the other.

I think that this walk through the Dark Valley was the worst part of little Christian's pilgrimage. Although he tried to think of the King and His goodness he could not help being frightened. And in one part of the valley, where some of the Wicked Prince's servants were waiting to trouble the pilgrims, a man came up behind him and whispered bad words in his ear. Little Christian could not see the man, and he was so confused that he fancied that he had said the wicked words himself, and he feared that the King would be angry with him.

About the middle of the night, as he was walking slowly along in the darkness, he heard footsteps in the distance. Some people were coming toward him, shouting and uttering dreadful cries. He knew that it must be a band of the Wicked Prince's servants, and he thought, *They will hurt me and perhaps kill me altogether.* He wondered whether he should turn back, for he was becoming so frightened that his whole body was trembling. But he had already come a long distance through the valley, and he said to himself, "Perhaps I am not far from the end of it, and going back might be worse than going forward." Presently he found that the wicked soldiers had taken a different path, and he did not meet them at all.

And now little Christian was comforted in his loneliness by hearing the voice of a pilgrim who was repeating aloud some of the beautiful words that were written in the King's Book. It was too dark for him to see who the pilgrim was, but he hoped that it might be Faithful and that he would soon be able to overtake him. At last he called out to him, but although Faithful heard Christian speak, he did not know who might be wishing to stop him, so he made no answer. Still, little Christian knew he was there, and he felt less frightened than when he had thought he was alone.

22

Little Christian
Overtakes Faithful

*L*ittle Christian had no rest that night. He did not dare to lie
down and sleep in the Dark Valley, for he feared lest the
wicked soldiers, whom he could hear passing up and down
among the rocks, should find him and put him to death or
carry him back to the City of Destruction. He was very tired,
but he walked bravely on through the mist and darkness,
praying in his heart that the King would watch over him. And
after a time he thought of some words that he had read in the
King's Book, "He shall give his angels charge over thee."

Then he remembered the picture that Charity loved so
much—of the little child with the Guardian Angel.

"The picture was true," he said to himself. "That little
child was walking on a path like this, and the King's angel
was taking care of him. Perhaps there is an angel with me
now!"

I am sure you know that little Christian was quite right. The angel had been with him all through that dreadful night, and although the little pilgrim could not see his bright guardian, there were gentle hands spread out to shield him from the terrors of the way, and strong arms ready to hold him fast if his feet slipped on the dangerous path.

At last the mist began to roll away, and a soft, pale light shone overhead. Little Christian looked up and found that he could now see a strip of sky between the overhanging rocks, and he knew that the day was breaking. As the sun rose and its glorious rays streamed even into the Dark Valley, he stood still and looked behind him. The black rocks that surrounded him, and the narrow track with the treacherous marsh on one side and the steep precipice on the other, seemed more fearful than they had been in the darkness. Little Christian wondered how he had ever come safely through such a dreadful place.

Then he looked forward and felt more and more thankful that the sun had risen, for he saw that the rest of the path was strewn with snares and nets, which the wicked soldiers had laid there to hinder and hurt the King's pilgrims. They had also dug holes in dangerous places and had done everything they could to make the road difficult and unsafe, so that Christian thought, *If I had passed over it in the darkness I should very likely have fallen and lamed myself.*

At the end of the Dark Valley there was a large cave in the side of the mountain, and in this cave two very powerful giants had once lived. Whenever pilgrims passed by their dwelling the giants attacked them and tried to kill them, and for a long time this was one of the most dangerous places on the way to the Celestial City. But one of the giants died, and the other grew old, and his limbs became stiff, so that he could no longer rush out upon the pilgrims.

When little Christian came near to the cave, he saw the old giant sitting outside it. He felt a little frightened, but the giant did not move, so he walked straight on. The giant was full of rage when he saw him, and he would have liked to seize the boy and drag him into his cave, but he had no strength left, and little Christian passed on safely.

The Dark Valley, with all its terrors, now lay behind him, and just before him the ground rose a little. Christian climbed quickly up the path, and when he reached the top of the ascent he found that he could see for some distance along the road.

Not very far from him a boy was walking with his face toward the King's City. He was wearing a white suit, like Christian's own, but he had no armor.

It must be Faithful, thought Christian, and he called out, "Wait for me, and I will walk with you." Then Faithful looked around, and Christian cried again, "Wait till I can overtake you."

But Faithful answered, "I am going to the King, and there are enemies behind me."

When Christian saw that Faithful would not wait for him he felt vexed, and he began to run as fast as he could. He soon caught Faithful, and instead of stepping by his side he ran on farther, so that Faithful, in his turn, might be left behind. But he forgot to look where he was going, and, striking his foot against a stone, he fell to the ground, and Faithful had to hurry after him and help him to get up.

23

Faithful Tells the Story of His Pilgrimage

*T*he two boys were very pleased to see each other, for they had been friends when they were living in the City of Destruction. Faithful had always been quiet and thoughtful, and he and little Christian had sometimes talked together about the King's Book and the wonderful stories that the strangers had told them.

"I am glad I have caught up with you," said Christian. "It will be much nicer to travel together."

"I meant to come all the way with you," replied Faithful, "but you went off so suddenly that I did not know until you were gone."

"How long did you stay in the City?"

"Only two or three days. After you left, the boys talked a great deal about the King's messages, but I don't think they really believed them."

"What did they say to Pliable?"

"Oh, they soon found out where he had been, for he was all over mud when he came back. They laughed at him and would not let him play with them."

"They need not have laughed at him," said little Christian. "*They* would not come."

"No, but they teased him for turning back at the first bit of trouble he came to. I met him the day after, and I was going to ask him about you, but he crossed over the street and pretended he didn't see me."

"I am very sorry," said Christian. "I thought he would be a real pilgrim, and it was a pity that he went home again. Now, tell me all that has happened to you."

"I did not fall into the Slough," said Faithful, "but I met a girl named Pleasure before I came to the Wicket-gate. She is a servant in the Wicked Prince's palace, and when she saw where I was going she tried to make me go back with her. I was afraid she *would* make me, for she was tall and strong. but I would not listen to what she said, and at last she told me I was a stupid boy and not worth speaking to."

Little Christian remembered how he had turned aside when Worldly deceived him, and he said, "You may be very glad you did not listen to her. Did you meet anyone else?"

"Not for some time. When I came to the Hill Difficulty, I saw a very old man sitting by the side of the road. He asked me whether I was going to the Celestial City, and he said I had much better come and live with him, for he would be good to me, and when he died I should have all his riches. He was so pleasant that I could not help listening to him, and he almost persuaded me to go with him."

"Oh," cried little Christian, "he would have taken you to the Wicked Prince!"

"Yes, I am sure he would. I was just ready to turn back, but I looked up and saw that he was smiling to himself. Then it came into my mind that perhaps he was one of the Wicked Prince's servants. So I said, 'I will not go.' Then he was very angry and told me he would send someone after me to hurt me. However, I escaped from him and went up the hill."

"Did he send anyone?" asked Christian.

"Yes. Just when I was passing that little arbor I heard someone coming quickly behind me. It was one of the King's servants, and he said he had come to punish me for listening to the old man. His name was Justice, and I thought he would have killed me with his rod, but a Man came by with a gentle face, and He told Justice not to strike me again. I did not know who it was at first, but when He was going up the hill I saw the marks upon His feet, and I am sure it must have been our dear Prince Himself."

"I have heard about Justice," said Christian, "but the Prince does not let him punish the pilgrims too much. Did you not see the palace at the top of the hill?"

"Yes, and the lions, too. They were asleep, and it was quite early, so I thought it was better to go on my way."

"The porter told me he had seen you. I wish you had stayed at the palace! The people are so kind. Did you meet anyone in the valley?"

"I met Discontent there, and he was very tiresome indeed."

"You did not meet Self?"

"No."

"*I* did," said Christian, "and he very nearly killed me."

24

Talkative

*T*he boys went on, talking happily together, until they came to a part of the plain in which the Way of the King was wider than usual. Faithful happened to turn his head, and he saw that another boy was walking on the opposite side of the road. He was a fine-looking lad, and Faithful thought that he might be a pleasant companion, so he said, "Are you going to the Celestial City?"

The boy answered, "Yes."

"Then let us walk together," said Faithful. "We are all traveling the same way."

"I shall like that very much," replied the boy, and he crossed over the road and began to talk with Faithful.

He had a great deal to say about the King and His servants and His laws, and little Faithful felt quite pleased to think of having a new friend who was so good and clever.

Presently he waited for Christian, who was walking a little way behind them, and whispered, "Is he not a nice boy? I am sure he must be a very good pilgrim."

Little Christian smiled.

"Don't you know who he is?" he asked.

"No," said Faithful. "I have not seen him before."

"Haven't you? Why, he lives in our city. His name is Talkative. He often pretends to be a pilgrim, just to amuse himself. But I did not know that he ever came as far as this."

"Is he a bad pilgrim, then?"

"I am afraid he does not love the King," said Christian, "but you will soon find out."

Then Faithful ran on again and walked by the side of Talkative.

Perhaps, thought the little pilgrim, *he may not be quite so bad as Christian thinks, and we may be able to persuade him to go with us.*

But the more the boy talked the less Faithful liked him, and at last he became quite sure that they could never be friends. It was plain that Talkative was very vain and foolish, and although he praised the King and said how delightful it was to be His servant, Faithful could see that he had no real wish to enter the Celestial City and that he was only pretending to be a pilgrim for the sake of amusing himself.

Faithful listened quietly for some time, while his companion talked about the King's goodness, and then he said, "I suppose you are very careful to obey all the King's laws?"

Talkative blushed, for he knew he always did just what he liked, although he was very ready to tell his friends what the King had commanded *them* to do.

He felt vexed with little Faithful for asking him such a question and answered crossly, "I don't see that it matters to you."

"I think it *does* matter," replied Faithful. "If you talk so much about loving the King, you ought to serve Him very well indeed."

"How do you know that I don't serve Him?" returned Talkative.

"I am not sure," said Faithful, "but I am afraid you don't.

"I wonder what a little fellow like you has to do with correcting *me*," cried Talkative, in an angry tone. "I am much older than you are!"

"I didn't mean to correct you at all, but I was not sure if you were a real pilgrim."

"A real pilgrim! Of course I am! But I know exactly how it is—Christian told you a lot of stories about me when you ran back to speak to him, and I suppose you believe them all."

Faithful did not know what to say, for he could see that Talkative was very angry indeed, so he walked on quietly without speaking.

"I don't care at all," said Talkative presently. "If you choose to believe bad things about me, it's your fault, not mine. But I think you are a very rude, disagreeable little boy, and I don't wish to talk to you anymore. You can just walk by yourself and leave me to do as I like."

He seemed so angry that Faithful made no answer. He let him go on his way alone and waited for Christian, who soon came up to him.

"Never mind," said Christian, when he heard what had happened. "I am glad he has not stayed with us, for I don't think he would have done us any good."

25

The Little Pilgrims Meet Evangelist

Soon after they had parted from Talkative the two little pilgrims came to a wide and desolate plain. No trees grew upon it, and there were no flowers among the short dry grass. The Way of the King went straight across it, and as Christian looked forward he felt glad that he was not alone, for the path looked long and dreary. But with Faithful for a companion the time passed quickly, and toward the close of the afternoon the tired children were glad to find that they were not very far from the border of the plain. Beyond it the country appeared green and beautiful, and Christian hoped that they might soon come to another one of the King's houses, where they would be allowed to rest until the morning.

Presently Faithful thought he heard footsteps behind him, and, looking back, he saw someone whose face seemed like that of an old friend.

He stood still for a minute, and then he cried out, "Oh, Christian, Christian! Do you see who is coming after us?"

Christian turned also and clapped his hands for joy.

"It is Evangelist!" he exclaimed.

How pleased the boys were to see their good friend once more! Evangelist had much to hear, and he smiled at the eagerness with which the little pilgrims told him of all that they had seen and done.

"The King has been very good to you," he said at length. "You have met with some enemies and some troubles, but He has helped you always, and He will help you still if you trust in Him."

"I am sure He will," said Christian.

Faithful only clasped his fingers a little more tightly round those of Evangelist, for he felt shy and half afraid to speak. But Evangelist knew that he loved and trusted the King with all his heart and that he would be quite as brave as Christian if the servants of the Wicked Prince were to attack him.

"Will you tell us more about the road?" asked Christian. "Will it be easier now, or are there some other dreadful places to pass through?"

Evangelist looked grave.

"I came to meet you here," he answered, "because very soon you will reach the gates of a great city that belongs to the Wicked Prince. It is a beautiful city, full of all kinds of pleasant things, and many pilgrims, when they enter it, are tempted to stay there instead of going on their journey. I do not wish you to be so foolish, so I have come to warn you about it."

"Why must we pass through it?" said Faithful.

"The Wicked Prince ordered it to be built on both sides of the King's Way, so that pilgrims cannot possibly get to the Celestial City without passing through the very middle of it."

"What shall we do, then?"

"You must walk quietly along the streets. Do not stop to look at the beautiful things in the shops and in the market, and do not let the children persuade you to play with them. Sometimes the pilgrims are not much troubled by the towns-people, and sometimes they are treated very cruelly."

"Would they *kill* us, do you think?" asked Christian.

"They may, perhaps, put you in prison," replied Evangelist, "and they often have been wicked enough to kill people who would not serve their Prince. But do not be afraid. If you have to die there, the King will send His angels, and they will carry you at once to the Celestial City, and you will have no more trouble or pain forever."

The sun was just setting when Evangelist told the children good-bye, and before its light had faded away they saw in the distance the walls and gates of a great and strong city.

"Are you afraid?" said little Christian.

"Not *very* much," answered Faithful. "The King will take care of us, and you have your good armor."

"Yes, I do wish that you had stayed at the Palace Beautiful. Then you would have had some armor, too."

"Never mind," said Faithful. "I shall keep close to you, and if the people *do* kill me, there will be no more enemies to fight."

He put his hand in Christian's, and Christian thought of the King and tried not to feel frightened. But he was only a little boy, and as he passed under the wide archway and heard the heavy gates close behind them, he whispered to Faithful, "I should like Evangelist to be taking hold of my hand now!"

And Faithful said, "Yes. Perhaps if we had asked him he would have gone through the city with us. What a pity we did not think of it!"

26

Vanity Fair

You know that the Wicked Prince hated the good King who ruled over the Celestial City, and it made him very angry to see the pilgrims on their way from his country to that of the King. He had built this city, which was called Vanity Fair, just beyond the Dark Valley and the wilderness, because he knew that when the pilgrims reached its gates they would be feeling tired and faint, and he hoped that it would then be easy to persuade them to stay there, instead of going farther on the Way of the King.

So he filled the great city with everything that was pleasant and beautiful. It had broad streets and handsome houses, and the stalls in its market were covered with glittering wares. All day long the people were passing busily up and down. They wore fine clothes and spent their whole time in pleasing themselves, and the Wicked Prince took care to give them plenty of things to enjoy so that they might never have a moment to spare in which to think of the King whom they had forsaken.

After they had lived in Vanity Fair for a short time most of the pilgrims used to forget the King altogether, and when they saw other pilgrims passing on their way to the Celestial City they were ready to help the servants of the Wicked Prince in persuading the travelers to give up their journey.

It was dark when our two little pilgrims entered the town, so they stayed quietly in a sheltered corner near to the gate until the next morning.

As soon as the sun rose they began their walk through the city, for they thought that if they started early they might, perhaps, reach the opposite gate before the streets became crowded with people.

But little Christian's bright armor and the white suit that Faithful wore were not like the dress of the children in Vanity Fair. And the boys had only gone a very short distance before they were noticed by some lads who were strolling idly about.

"There are two little pilgrims," they cried. "Let us go after them and stop them."

Christian and Faithful could hear the boys running behind them, but they did not look around.

"Don't let us take any notice," said Christian. "Perhaps they will only just speak to us."

But when the boys came up, they all gathered closely round the little pilgrims and would not let them pass.

"Tell us where you have come from," said one.

"And who gave you that armor and those white clothes?" cried another.

"Why don't you look at the shops?" asked a third. "Boys like you don't want swords and shields! You should sell them and buy some of these beautiful things."

Christian scarcely knew what to say, for the boys were all speaking at once, and he felt quite confused. But little Faithful answered bravely, "We don't wish for any of your things—we are going to the Celestial City."

Then the boys laughed rudely, and one of them pushed Faithful so that he would have fallen if he had not been holding Christian's hand.

By this time many older children had run toward them, and some other people stopped also to see what was the matter. Then one of the Wicked Prince's servants passed by, and when he saw Christian's shining helmet he knew that the boys must be pilgrims. So he pushed his way through the crowd and seized them both by their shoulders.

"What are you doing?" he asked. "Our Prince does not allow children to quarrel in his streets."

"We are not quarreling," said Christian. "We were walking along quietly."

"That is nonsense," replied the man. "You have caused all this crowd and disturbance. You must come with me."

"We are the King's pilgrims," said Faithful. "We are not disturbing anybody. We only wish to pass through the city."

"I don't know anything about the King's pilgrims," answered the man. "I can see that you are two foolish, troublesome boys, and you must be taken before the Governor."

So he led them both down the street to the Governor's house, and the children of the town followed, laughing and mocking at the poor little pilgrims, whom they had brought into such trouble.

27

The Little Pilgrims Suffer
for the King's Sake

*T*he Governor of the city was one of the Wicked Prince's chief servants, and he hated the King and His pilgrims almost as much as his master did.

When Faithful and little Christian were brought before him, he was quite glad to think that he had an excuse for hurting someone whom the King loved, and he said, "You are two very bad boys, and you must both be beaten and afterward you shall be shut up in the iron cage, so that the children of the town may see you and know what will be done to them if they follow your example."

It was no use for the little pilgrims to say anything. The tears came into Christian's eyes when he heard the Governor's cruel words, and he wondered whether his mother would know what was happening to him.

Faithful's cheeks grew very white, but he whispered to Christian, "Evangelist said that they might hurt us, but if we die we shall go straight to the Celestial City. I shall think of the King, because He is sure to help me, and I will not cry."

Then Christian determined to be brave too, and he remembered the picture he had seen in the house of the Interpreter, of the Good Shepherd, whose feet were torn and bleeding.

He is our Prince, thought Christian, *and* He *did not mind the pain. I must not, either, because I am the King's servant, and it is written in my Book that the King's servants are to be like the Prince.* And, although the strokes of the heavy rod made his back and arms feel terribly sore and bruised, he behaved like a brave soldier and did not cry at all.

The iron cage was a place in the middle of the market, with bars of iron in front of it, so that it looked like a den for wild beasts. After they had been beaten, the little pilgrims had chains fastened upon their hands and feet, and then the man who had charge of them put them into the cage and left them there.

They could not stand upright, for they were ill and weak with pain, so they sat down together upon the ground, and each tried to comfort the other by reminding him of the King's promises.

"We knew that they would be cruel," said Faithful, "but it is for the King's sake, and He will not let them hurt us too much."

When the people in the town heard that two of the King's pilgrims were lying in the cage, they were very eager to see them, and soon a crowd of rude boys and girls, and men and women also, gathered round to stare at Faithful and Christian and to mock them in their trouble.

The boys of Vanity Fair said all kinds of cruel things to provoke the pilgrims and to make them displease the King by being passionate and angry with their enemies. But Christian and Faithful sat still, and neither of them gave a cross answer to anything that was said.

At last some of the boys, when they saw how patient the little pilgrims were, began to feel ashamed, and they cried out, "Let them alone now. They have been beaten, and it is brave of them not to cry. Don't tease them anymore."

But the other boys were cruel, and liked to see the white faces and trembling lips of the poor little pilgrims. So they went on teasing them and laughing at them until their companions grew angry, and before long there was a great disturbance in the market, for the boys who were sorry for the pilgrims began to fight with those who were teasing them.

The Governor was obliged to send his men to stop the fighting, and he ordered Christian and Faithful to be beaten once more, because he said the quarrel had been on their account. Then they were taken back to the cage, where they lay all night in great pain and distress.

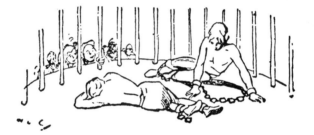

28

Faithful Ends His Pilgrimage

When the morning came, Christian and Faithful were taken to the Governor's Court, where the judge sat every day to try any prisoners who might be brought to him. He was an old man, with a hard and cruel face, and like the Governor he hated the King and all His pilgrims.

Christian and Faithful were brought before him with their hands chained, and he asked where they had come from and what they had been doing.

Then a boy named Envy, who had been one of the first to run after the little pilgrims and tease them, rose up and began to answer the judge's questions. He said he had known Christian and Faithful when they were living at home and that they were disobedient and quarrelsome and did not honor the Wicked Prince, who was the ruler of their country.

Two other boys followed Envy, and they agreed that what he had said was quite true. They also told the judge that they were afraid the pilgrims would do great harm to the children of Vanity Fair if they were allowed to be at liberty, because they laughed at the treasures with which the Wicked Prince had filled the city, saying they were not worth having, and they pretended that they knew of a finer city and another King, whose laws were better than those of the Wicked Prince.

There were twelve men sitting in the court, whose duty it was to listen to everything that was said about the prisoners and then help the judge to decide whether they deserved punishment or not. These twelve men were called the jury. Of course they were chosen from among the chief servants of the Wicked Prince and were not likely to be kind or just to any of the King's pilgrims.

However, they always pretended to treat their prisoners fairly, so when Faithful asked if he might speak to them, the judge answered, "You ought to be put to death at once for all that you have done, but we will first hear what you have to say."

Christian wondered how it was that Faithful had become so brave. His face was pale, but he did not seem to be frightened, although the judge and the people in the court looked wicked and cruel. Christian afterward knew that the King had helped His little pilgrim and had made the timid boy brave and strong, so that he was not afraid to speak out and own that he loved his King dearly and would obey no one else.

When Faithful had spoken, the judge turned to the jury and said, "You have heard what Envy and his companions have told us about these boys, and Faithful does not deny it. He will not serve our Prince, and by the laws of our city he ought to be put to death."

Then the twelve men answered, "We can see that both these pilgrims are wicked boys, but Faithful is the worst, because he is not ashamed to speak against our Prince. We think that he must be killed, but Christian can be taken back to prison."

Poor little Christian's mind had been so troubled by all that had happened that he scarcely understood what the jury was saying, and when the soldiers of the Wicked Prince came in and led Faithful out of the court, he wondered where they were going. In a few minutes he, too, was taken into the marketplace, and there he saw his companion in the midst of those cruel men, who were beating him and wounding him with their sharp weapons.

"Oh, Faithful! Faithful!" he cried out, but Faithful did not answer. He was looking up into the sky, and his face was shining with a beautiful light, like the face of Christian's mother had shone when he saw her in his dream.

Then Christian looked up also, and in the air just above the place where Faithful was standing, he could see a band of angels with their wings outspread, and he knew that they were waiting to carry the soul of the little pilgrim to its home in the Celestial City.

29

Little Christian Leaves Vanity Fair

*L*ittle Christian knew that the angels would carry Faithful safely into the presence of the King, and as he thought of this he forgot for a moment that he was in the midst of Vanity Fair, surrounded by the servants of the Wicked Prince. Suddenly the boys of the city gave a great shout of pleasure, because they loved to see a little pilgrim punished, and their cry startled Christian, so that he turned once more to look at his lost friend.

But the King is very merciful, and He did not wish Christian to know how much poor Faithful was suffering. A mist seemed to pass before his eyes, and he cried out again, "Oh, Faithful! Faithful!" Then a strange feeling came over him, and he fancied that his mother had pushed her way through the crowd and had lifted him in her arms and carried him away into an open space, where there were no soldiers and no noisy, mocking children.

There he lay for some time, feeling too weak to move or speak. But presently he opened his eyes and found that he was in the prison, upon a little bed, and that a woman was bending over him. She was gaily dressed, like all women in Vanity Fair, and, although she did not look unkind, her face was very different from that of Christian's mother. She was the wife of the man who kept the prison, and when the little fainting boy had been carried from the marketplace by the soldier who had taken charge of him she had been sorry to see him. So she brought some water and bathed his hands and face gently and stayed by him until he revived.

"You poor little child!" she said, presently. "You are too young to be a pilgrim. I should like to keep you here and take care of you."

"You are very kind to me," he said, "but I could not stay. I am going to the King."

"Ah!" replied the woman. "I was going to the King once, but the way was hard, and I have been very happy here in the city."

"You would be happier with the King," said Christian. "Faithful is gone—I saw the angels waiting for him. And if they ever let me out of prison, I shall travel as fast as I can to the end of my journey."

The woman stroked the boy's hair softly. "Faithful is dead," she whispered. "I was sorry when they told me, but they are not going to kill you."

"I don't think I would have minded," said Christian, "for then I should have gone straight to the Celestial City, and now, perhaps, I shall be kept here always, or, if not, I shall have to go the rest of the way alone."

"They will only keep you in prison for a few days," answered the woman. "Stay with me. I will be very kind to you."

But Christian shook his head. "I couldn't stay. I love the King, and I must go to Him."

After a few days the keeper of the prison came to him and told him that the Governor of the city had given an order for him to be set free, so Christian started once more on his journey. The kind woman was sorry to see him go, and she kissed him and bade him think of her sometimes.

"I will tell the King how good you have been to me," said Christian, "and perhaps, some day, you will be a pilgrim again. If I see you coming into the Celestial City I shall know you."

He went quietly down the street, not feeling strong enough yet to walk quickly and fearing very much lest the boys should run after him, as they had done before. But as Faithful had been put to death they were satisfied, and although they laughed together when the little pale-faced pilgrim passed they did not touch or interfere with him in any way.

He was just going through the great archway of the city gate when he heard someone running behind him, and then he felt a hand upon his shoulder. For a minute he was frightened, thinking that his troubles were beginning again, but the boy who had stopped him looked frightened too and said in a half whisper, "Let me come with you. I don't want to stay here any longer."

"Do you mean that you will be a pilgrim?" said Christian.

"Yes. I am called Hopeful, and I want to go with you. But wait until we are safely on the road, and then I will tell you all about it."

30

By-ends

*C*hristian tried to walk a little faster, and Hopeful kept close to him, but he seemed afraid to speak until they were some distance from the city.

Then he said, "We were sorry, you know, because they killed Faithful. He was so brave, and I am sure he was good. And there are some more boys and girls, too, who say that they will not stay in the city much longer if such cruel things are done there. I was just passing the prison when you came out, and I watched you, and then, when no one was looking, I ran after you. You don't mind my coming, do you?"

"Not if you really love the King," replied Christian. "I thought I should have to go the rest of the way by myself, and I shall be very glad indeed if you will come too."

"Yes, I will come," said Hopeful. "I wasn't happy, and I always meant to run away some day."

Christian was just beginning to ask how long Hopeful had been living in Vanity Fair when they overtook another boy, who was strolling very slowly on the sunny side of the road. He came from a city not far from Vanity Fair. The people who lived in it called themselves the King's servants and pretended to love Him very much. But whenever the Wicked Prince or his servants came to see them they left off talking about the King and behaved as if the Wicked Prince were their ruler. The Wicked Prince liked these people, and when he heard that any of them had become pilgrims he never tried to hinder them in their journey, because he knew that they would be sure to turn back again as soon as they met with the least difficulty or danger.

The boy, whose name was By-ends, joined Christian and Hopeful and walked with them for a short time. He told them that all his relations and friends were very rich people. And he seemed proud of his high position and inclined to despise Christian and Hopeful.

"Isn't it a beautiful day?" said Hopeful presently, for the sun was shining brightly, and the breeze was soft and pleasant.

"Yes," replied By-ends. "It is just nice for traveling. But pilgrims from our city never start in the winter. We always choose clear summer weather for our journeys. It is foolish to tire yourself with struggling against wind and rain."

"There are storms even in the summer," said Christian.

"You needn't travel in them. If it began to rain I should creep under a thick bush until it was fine again."

Christian could not help smiling, but he answered, "I am sure good pilgrims never do that. We ought not to mind about the weather."

"Well, of course," said By-ends, "you can do as you like. We need not quarrel about it. If there is a storm, you can walk in it if you choose, but I shall certainly wait until it is over."

Now Christian had read in his Book that it is unwise for pilgrims to have friends who are not the King's true servants, so he said, "I am afraid if you think in that way we shall not be good companions for you. We must go straight on, whether it is fine or stormy."

"Very well," answered By-ends. "You had better go on by yourselves. I was very happy before you came, and I'm sure I don't want you to stay with me!"

"It was a pity to vex him," said Christian, as he walked on with Hopeful, "but I don't see how we could help it. If we stayed with him, and there happened to be a storm, he might persuade us to turn back altogether."

By-ends had really been feeling rather lonely and was very glad when Christian and Hopeful overtook him. But he was too idle and fond of his own comfort to be willing to serve the King faithfully, as they wished to do. He put his hands in his pockets and tried to look as if he did not care when they left him, although he felt almost inclined to run after them and say that he did not mind about storms any more than they did.

It wouldn't matter, he thought. *They couldn't make me go any farther than I wished, no matter how much I promised them. They are silly boys, but their company would be better than none.*

But before By-ends had made up his mind what to do, he heard shouts behind him, and turning around he saw three of his schoolfellows beckoning to him to wait for them.

"Where are you off to?" they cried, as they came up to him.

"There wasn't anything particular to do at home," said By-ends, "so I thought I'd see how I like being a pilgrim."

"We'll go with you. Who are those two boys in front? We saw you talking to them."

"Oh, they are pilgrims, too," replied By-ends, "but not *our* sort. They are servants of the King. I told them I should only travel while the weather kept fine; so they said I might stay by myself. I don't see the use of plodding over rough roads in wind and rain. You may just as well stop until the storm is over."

"Of course," said one of the boys, "but the King's servants are always like that, and if you don't exactly agree to everything they say, they won't have anything to do with you. However, what does it matter? Let them alone, and we shall be a nice little party, all to ourselves."

31

Demas and the Silver Mine

By-ends and his schoolfellows walked on together, laughing and talking. Christian and Hopeful were not very far from them, and presently the four boys ran after them and began to ask them foolish questions.

They pretended that they wished to know whether some of the things that they were fond of doing were wrong and likely to displease the King, and they hoped that Christian would not be brave enough to answer them truly, because then they would be able to call him a coward. But although little Christian was a shy and timid child, he was not afraid to speak the truth. He had learned to love the King dearly, and no fear of what these rough boys might do to him would have made him agree with By-ends and his friends.

He answered all their questions bravely and truly, and at last they began to feel ashamed of themselves and said no more. Christian was very glad when they left him, and he went on with Hopeful, while By-ends stayed behind with his three idle companions.

Very soon the little pilgrims came to a narrow plain, where the pathway was smooth and easy. And just beyond it they saw a hill, with an opening in its side, like the mouth of a cave. A lad was standing upon the hill, and when Christian and Hopeful passed by he called to them saying, "Come up here, and I will show you something."

"What is it?" said Christian.

"A mine of silver," said the lad. "It is full of rich treasure, and you can soon gather up enough to take with you on your journey."

"Oh," cried Hopeful, "let us go and look at it!"

But Christian pulled him back. "No, no!" he said. "It is not a safe place." Then he called to the lad, whose name was Demas, and asked him if it were not dangerous.

Demas knew quite well that it was very dangerous indeed. But he was a servant of the Wicked Prince, to whom the mine belonged, and he had been sent there on purpose to tempt the pilgrims by telling them of its rich store of silver. So he answered, "It is safe unless you are very careless."

But Christian turned away, saying to Hopeful, "We will not go. I am sure I have heard about it, and you see we could not reach it without leaving the Way of the King."

Then Demas cried, "If you will not come, you might at least wait for me, and I will go with you. I am a pilgrim, too."

"I don't think you are one of the King's pilgrims," replied Christian, "or you would not try to hinder us in our journey. We cannot wait for anybody."

So Demas said no more but watched for By-ends and the other boys, who were not far off. Hopeful turned round to see what they would do. They did not love the King, and they did not care at all about the Celestial City to which they pretended they were going. So when they heard of the treasure hidden in the hillside they hurried eagerly to the mouth of the cave. Demas knew that people who went into it to dig for silver were nearly always either lost or killed there, but he told By-ends and his friends that it was quite safe, and they were ready to believe everything that he said.

Christian and Hopeful saw them enter the cave, but no one ever heard anything of them again. No doubt they ventured too far along the dark and winding passages and were never able to find their way back into the daylight.

When the little pilgrims had walked for some distance beyond the hill, Hopeful stopped suddenly, saying, "Oh, what can that be?"

Christian looked where he pointed and saw a strange white figure standing by the roadside. As they came nearer, the boys saw that it did not move and that it was in the shape of a woman, with her face turned away from the Celestial City.

"Do you think she was a pilgrim?" whispered Hopeful.

"I don't know," said Christian. "It looks like a statue. I wonder why it is placed here by the wayside."

They walked around it and looked at it carefully. At last Hopeful saw a few words carved upon the border of the woman's veil, just where it lay upon her forehead. They were old and worn, and he could not make them out, but after puzzling over them a little, Christian read them—

"REMEMBER LOT'S WIFE."

"I know what it is now," he said. "I read about it in the library at the Palace Beautiful."

Then he told Hopeful how the King had once rescued a man named Lot, with his wife and two daughters, from a city which was being destroyed for its wickedness.

"He sent an angel to bring them out, and the angel told them not to look back. But Lot's wife *did* look back, and the moment she turned, her body grew quite stiff, and she became a pillar of salt, so that she could never move again."

"What a dreadful thing!" said Hopeful. "Is it put here to frighten us?"

"Not to frighten us, I think, but to make us careful. I am very glad we did not go up the hill when Demas called us."

"So am I, for I should not like the King to punish *me*."

32

The Valley of Peace

The two boys were obliged to travel very slowly that day, on account of Christian's weakness.

"Where shall we sleep?" said Hopeful. "You cannot walk all night, and it will not be safe to lie down by the wayside."

"Perhaps there is another house like the Palace Beautiful," replied Christian. "I *was* happy there! You cannot think how kind Discretion and her daughters were to me."

Then Hopeful began to ask questions about them, and Christian tried to tell him of all that he had seen and heard at the palace. But the little pilgrim's strength was failing after the day's journey. He soon became too tired to speak and could scarcely walk, even with the help of Hopeful's arm. Hopeful was kind and gentle and did all he could to cheer his weary little companion. But he began to feel very anxious when he saw that Christian's face was growing paler and paler every minute.

If we could only find a place to rest in, he thought. And as the evening shadows closed round the pathway he strained his eyes eagerly in the hope of seeing some distant light, which would tell him that they were coming near to a house where they might stay until the morning.

But no light appeared, and presently the night came on, and still the little pilgrims crept slowly along, for Christian would not be persuaded to lie down upon the grass, although Hopeful promised to watch carefully by his side.

"We will go on," he said. "I don't think the King will forget us. He knows how tired we are, and He will be sure to give rest soon."

And now the stars began to twinkle in the dark sky, and the moon rose over the hills and shed her pure soft light upon the Way of the King. As Hopeful looked forward he saw that the pathway was widening and that a broad river was flowing in the distance.

"We are coming to a beautiful country!" he exclaimed. "Look, Christian! The river is close to the wayside, and the path must lead through that meadow, which is all fenced in and safe."

Christian looked, and the sight of the river and the hope of resting revived him a little. In a short time they reached the brink of the water and found that Hopeful was right. The Way of the King ran close to the river, which was called the River of Life, and the ground on both sides of it was protected by strong fences, forming a beautiful meadow covered with soft grass and flowers and shaded by tall, spreading trees, under whose boughs the King's pilgrims might rest safely and have no fear of enemies.

How thankful Christian was to lay his aching little body upon a mossy bank! Hopeful sat by him and watched the moonlight playing peacefully upon the rippling water.

Soon he clasped Christian's hand, saying, "The Wicked Prince never comes here."

"Oh, no!" said Christian. "I am sure he does not. It is all so still and happy!"

The little pilgrims lay down side by side and slept quietly until the morning. When the sun rose, a messenger came to them from the King.

"This is the Valley of Peace," he said. "You are to stay for a few days, until Christian grows strong again. You will find plenty of food, for the trees are full of fruit, and you must drink the water of the river, which will strengthen and refresh you."

So the boys spent a whole week in the beautiful valley, resting and enjoying their life more and more every day. Christian was not afraid to loosen his armor in this quiet spot, and he would sit by the river, leaning comfortably against the trunk of some wide-spreading tree, while Hopeful lay on the grass near him, plucking the flowers or gathering up the delicious fruit, which was now ripe and falling from the heavily laden boughs.

After all Christian's troubles, the Valley of Peace seemed very pleasant. Soon the color came back to his cheeks and the strength to his limbs, and he felt able to continue his journey.

"I don't think we are *very* far from the Celestial City," he said, "and I shall be *so* glad when we get there! After this good rest we shall be able to travel faster."

33

By-path Meadow

*T*he little pilgrims left the Valley of Peace early in the morning and traveled along the Way of the King all that day. Late in the afternoon they came to a place where a stile led into a broad green meadow. It was called By-path Meadow, and it belonged to a cruel and powerful giant named Despair. He was one of the most famous soldiers in the Wicked Prince's army, and he lived in a strong castle beyond the meadow, which could not be seen from the Way of the King. This was all written in Christian's Book, but he did not think of looking at it just then.

The boys were both feeling very tired. They had found the path leading from the river rough and stony, and their feet were sore and aching.

Christian stopped when he saw the stile, and leaned over it. A fence divided the meadow from the Way of the King, but a smooth grassy path ran close to it.

"Could we not walk along this path for a little way?" he said, turning to Hopeful. "The stones are so hard, and my feet ache dreadfully."

"So do mine," answered Hopeful, "but would it be safe?" Then he came to the stile also and looked over.

"Oh, I think it must be," said Christian. "See, it runs close to the fence. We could climb back again anywhere in a minute."

Hopeful did not feel quite sure that they were doing right, but as he thought that Christian knew more about the King's laws than he did, he followed his companion into the meadow. The grass was soft and pleasant to their feet, and not far before them another boy was walking along near to the fence.

Christian called to him, saying, "Can you tell us where this path leads to?"

The boy, whose name was Vain-Confidence, turned round and replied, "To the Celestial City."

"You see," said Christian, "I was right. We shall be quite safe. We can keep behind that boy, and then, if there *is* any danger, we shall know of it in time to escape."

But Hopeful was not satisfied, and when the night came on and the shadows grew so thick that the figure of Vain-Confidence could no longer be seen, he felt frightened. Suddenly a cry was heard, and a sound of falling. Hopeful seized Christian's arm and clung to him in great fear, and Christian, too, lost his courage and began to tremble from head to foot.

"What can have happened?" he said, and he called again to Vain-Confidence, but he received no answer. Only, through the darkness, the boys could hear that someone was groaning as if in terrible pain.

"I am *sure* we are not in the right way," said Hopeful, "and it is so dark."

Christian did not answer. He knew now that he had done wrong in climbing over the stile, and he wondered how he could have been so foolish as to think that any path could be safe that led him out of the straight road.

But before he could speak again he felt some heavy drops of rain upon his face. Then a bright flash of lightning darted across the sky, and a roar of thunder followed. The rain poured in torrents, and the thunder and lightning were more fearful than any which they had heard or seen before.

Christian began to cry and to wish that he had not been so careless. "It was my fault," he said. "Oh, Hopeful, I am sorry! I deserve to be killed, but you would never have come if I had not persuaded you."

"I might have," said Hopeful, not liking to hear poor Christian's sobs. "Don't cry, Christian. It was my fault, too, because I didn't try to prevent your coming."

"Let us turn back," said Christian. "Perhaps we can find our way."

By this time the heavy rain had filled the little streams that ran through the meadow, and the path by the fence was flooded. The water was so deep that the boys could scarcely keep their footing, and they began to fear that they would never get back into the Way of the King.

The storm lasted for many hours, and although Christian and Hopeful struggled on bravely they soon found that it would not be possible to make their way to the stile in the darkness. So at last they crouched down together in a little sheltered corner close to the fence, meaning to watch for the first gleam of daylight and then hasten on their way. But they were both worn out with fright and weariness, and before the morning came they fell asleep.

34

Seized by the Giant

The storm passed away before daybreak, and the sun rose in a clear sky and shone brightly over the Way of the King. Christian and Hopeful were lying under the shadow of the fence and did not feel the warmth of the sunbeams. So, instead of making their way back to the stile in the early morning, as they had intended to do, they slept soundly and knew nothing of the danger that was close at hand.

Giant Despair had heard the storm raging, and he came down from his castle soon after sunrise and walked through his fields and meadows to see if any harm had been done by the wind and rain. Last of all, he crossed By-path Meadow and on his way home passed by the very spot where the little pilgrims were sleeping.

Hopeful's dress, which had once been white and new, had become soiled and shabby while he stayed in Vanity Fair; but Christian's armor still looked bright, although it was sadly splashed with the mud through which he had walked the night before. The Giant caught sight of his shining helmet among the bushes by the fence, and he turned at once to see who was lying there.

"They are pilgrims of the King," he said to himself, and he smiled to think that they were in his power.

A loud voice roused Christian from his dreams, and when he opened his eyes he saw the Giant stooping over him. Despair was a terrible-looking man, with shaggy hair and beard, and clothes made of the rough skins of wild beasts. Christian cried out with fear when he saw him, and this roused Hopeful, who sprang up trembling.

"What are you going here?" said the Giant.

"We are pilgrims," answered Christian, whose lips were quivering so that he could scarcely speak, "and we have lost our way."

"You have no right to sleep in my meadow," said the Giant, and his voice was so harsh and deep that the boys were more frightened by it than they had been by the storm. "I shall take you back with me to my castle."

The poor little pilgrims knew that they were quite helpless. If they had tried to run away this great strong man would have overtaken them in a moment. He drove them before him across the fields to his house, which was called Doubting Castle, and put them into a dark dungeon, locking the door behind him.

All day and all night they lay there upon the bare ground, without either food or water, and not even able to see each other. Hopeful crept close to Christian, and they clung together, wondering whether the Giant would soon come and put them to death. Christian's heart was very full of grief, because he felt that he had caused all this trouble. And now he feared that the Giant would kill them both and that they would never reach the Celestial City.

Giant Despair had a wife, whose name was Diffidence. He told her that he found two little pilgrims sleeping in his meadow and that he had brought them home and locked them up in one of his dungeons. Diffidence was very pleased to hear this, and, being a cruel woman, she said that she hoped her husband would beat his little prisoners. So in the morning the Giant took his club and went down to the dungeon.

When he had beaten the boys, he left them again in the darkness, and they were so bruised by the heavy blows that they could not move, but lay upon the ground all that day, moaning with pain.

The next day Despair visited them again and seemed surprised to find they they were not dead. He told them that he should never let them leave his castle, but that if they did not wish to die for want of food they might drink some poison that he would leave with them. Then Christian begged him to have mercy upon them and to set them free, and this made the Giant so angry that he rushed upon them with his club and would have killed them, but his strength suddenly failed, and he was obliged to leave them for that time. In the bright weather he often had fits of weakness and lost the use of his hands, so that sometimes the pilgrims whom he carried into his castle were able to escape from him.

Christian did not know this, and he began to think that it was now foolish to hope for deliverance.

"What shall we do?" he said. "If we are to stay here until we die, will it not be better to drink this poison than to die slowly for want of food?"

"I am sure we must not do that," said Hopeful. "If we were to kill ourselves, the angels would never come to take us to the Celestial City. They only come when the King sends them. Perhaps if the Giant is ill again he may forget to lock the door, and we may be able to slip out before his strength comes back. Let us wait a little longer, and the King may show us a way to escape."

35

The Key of Promise

*I*n the evening, the Giant came down into the dungeon again, hoping to find that his poor little prisoners were dead. But although they were very weak and faint, they were still alive, and they had not touched the poison that he had left with them. This made Despair very angry, and he frightened the children so much with his terrible looks and words that little Christian fainted quite away. When his senses returned, the Giant was gone, and only Hopeful sat by him, rubbing his hands and trying to keep him warm.

"I think we shall have to take the poison," he said. "It is dreadful here. We cannot bear it much longer, and we shall never be able to escape."

"You must not talk in that way," replied Hopeful. "You are forgetting all that has happened to you before. Just remember what a long way you have traveled and how many dangers you have been in. You were not afraid to fight with Self, and the King helped you to conquer him. You passed safely through the Dark Valley, and even in Vanity Fair the King did not let you be killed. Let us trust in Him and wait a little longer."

Now the Giant and his wife knew that pilgrims who killed themselves never went to the Celestial City. But if Despair killed them, the King always sent His angels to carry them away. So when Diffidence heard that the children were still alive she was no less angry than her husband.

"You had better take them into the courtyard tomorrow," she said, "and let them see the bones of the pilgrims who have died here before. Then perhaps they will be frightened and will drink the poison."

The Giant thought that this would be a good plan, and in the morning he brought Christian and Hopeful out of the dungeon and led them into the courtyard, which was strewn all over with the bones of men and women and even of little children. It was a very dreadful sight, and the Giant was pleased to see how frightened his little prisoners looked.

"These are the bones of pilgrims," he said. "They came into my meadows, as you did, and I brought them to my castle and killed them. In a few days I shall put you both to death like I have others, and your bones will lie here with the rest."

Then he beat them once more, and they lay all day in their dark prison, crying together and wondering whether their troubles would ever come to an end.

The same night, when Despair was talking to his wife, he said that he could not remember how it was that these two little boys were so very brave.

"Perhaps," replied Diffidence, "they think that someone will come to save them, or they may have a key hidden in their clothes, with which they will open the doors when we are not watching. You have lost prisoners in that way many times."

This was quite true, but the Giant thought that if Christian had had one of the King's keys with him he would have used it before. "But I will search them both in the morning," he said, and then he fell asleep.

The little key, which was called the Key of Promise, lay in Christian's pocket. It had been given to him at the Palace Beautiful, but in his trouble he had forgotten all about it.

Neither he nor Hopeful could sleep that night, and after talking together for some time they began to pray to the King and beg Him very earnestly to help them.

"He will hear us," said Christian, "though we cannot see Him, and I am beginning to feel as if we should escape after all."

The King did hear the little pilgrims' prayer, and He sent one of His bright angels to tell them what to do. They did not see the angel, but a thought came suddenly into Christian's mind, and that thought was really the whisper of the King's bright messenger.

"Oh, how stupid I have been!" he cried. "We have stayed here all these days, when we might have gone away at once. Discretion gave me a little key, and I believe it will open every one of the Giant's locks."

Hopeful sprang up. "Let us try it!" he said. "It must still be night, and no doubt Despair is asleep."

They felt carefully in the darkness until they found the lock of the dungeon door, and Christian put the key into it. It turned quite easily, and with beating hearts the boys stepped softly over the threshold and listened. A dim light shone down the passage, and they soon found their way to the door that led into the courtyard. This Christian opened also, and, not daring even to whisper, Hopeful followed him across the pavement. The moon was shining brightly, and only one more door stood between the little pilgrims and the green meadow.

But this last lock was very stiff, and although Christian tried with all his might he could not turn the key. Then the Giant's step sounded upon the castle stairs, for he had heard someone moving. The little pilgrims thought that he would overtake them, and they were ready to faint with fear. But just as Despair reached the doorway his club dropped from his hands, and he fell heavily upon the ground.

"Oh, *do* try harder!" cried Hopeful, "and we shall get away before his fit is over."

"I *am* trying," said Christian, "but the lock is rusty."

Hopeful put his hands also upon the key. "It is moving!" he said, and in another moment the lock gave way.

The Giant still lay upon the ground, and the boys hastily pulled back the heavy bolts and opened the door. Then Hopeful seized Christian's hand, and they ran as fast as they could across the broad meadow towards the stile that led into the Way of the King.

36

The Delectable Mountains

"*O*h," exclaimed Christian, when at last the boys found themselves once more on the Way of the King, "how glad I am that Discretion gave me the key!"

"Yes," said Hopeful, "what *should* we have done without it?"

They sat down together upon the roadside, for they were out of breath with running. They were not afraid to rest there, for they felt sure that Despair would not follow them into the King's Way.

"It is a pity that pilgrims do not know where that path will lead them," said Christian. "Could we not write something upon a stone and set it up near the stile?"

"We might try," replied Hopeful. "I can cut some letters, if we can find a stone."

They looked up and down and presently they found a large smooth block of stone lying in the grass.

"This will do very well," said Christian. "You can cut the letters first, and then I think we can push it into the right place."

So Hopeful drew out his knife, and after consulting together they carved these words upon the stone:

"This path leads to Doubting Castle, which belongs to Giant Despair. He is the King's enemy, and he tries to kill the pilgrims."

Hopeful was some time over his task, but at last it was finished, and before the moon went down the stone was pushed across the grass and placed close to the stile, so that no one could pass by without seeing it.

"It will perhaps save someone," said Hopeful. "It was a good thing that you thought of it."

The short summer night was soon over, and the sun rose behind the hills. The little pilgrims walked on quietly, enjoying the light and the fresh air very much after spending those terrible days and nights in the dungeon.

"What beautiful hills those are!" said Hopeful. "And the Way of the King leads over them."

"I think they must be the Delectable Mountains," replied Christian. "I saw them far away, when I was at the Palace Beautiful. I believe some Shepherds live there who are kind to the pilgrims. Perhaps they will give us some food and let us rest a little."

Very soon the children came close to the mountains and began to climb the pathway that led across them. It was not steep and rugged like that upon the Hill Difficulty. It was smooth and easy, and the slopes on each side of it were planted with vines. Little streams of pure water sparkled in the grass, and trees laden with fruit grew here and there, with spreading boughs that hung over the Way of the King, and it screened the pilgrims from the heat of the sun.

Christian and Hopeful were very hungry, and thirsty also, and they were glad to eat some of the fruit and to take a draught of the cool clear water.

The Shepherds were not far from the path, and when they saw the boys coming, four of their number went down the green slope to meet them.

"Are these the Delectable Mountains?" asked Christian.

"Yes," replied one of the Shepherds. "This country is called Immanuel's Land. It belongs to the Prince, and it is in sight of the King's City. These sheep are His, and we live upon the mountains to take care of them."

"Is it very far to the Celestial City?" asked Christian. "And is the way safe?"

"It is safe for those who love the King, but pilgrims who do not serve Him faithfully often fall into danger."

"Is there any place here where pilgrims may rest?" asked Christian. "We are both so *very* tired."

"Oh, yes!" replied the Shepherds. "The King has commanded us to do all that we can for any of His servants who pass over the mountains. Come to our tents, and we will take good care of you."

So the Shepherds, whose names were Knowledge, Experience, Watchful, and Sincere, led the children to their tents and brought them water to wash in and gave them plenty of wholesome food. Then, seeing how tired they were, Watchful prepared beds for them, where they slept comfortably and awoke early in the morning feeling refreshed and strengthened.

37

The Rock of Error
and Mount Caution

*T*he next day, when the little pilgrims were preparing to continue their journey, the Shepherds came to them and asked whether they would like to go for a walk upon the mountains before they went away.

Christian and Hopeful thought they would enjoy this very much, so the Shepherds went with them over the broad green slopes and along the paths that had been cut upon the sides of the hills.

"It is not safe," said Knowledge, "for strangers to walk across these mountains alone, but the King allows us to take some of the pilgrims to see the view of the Celestial City."

Presently they came to a steep path that was rugged and not very easy to climb. It led to the top of a great rock, and when they reached the highest point, Christian and Hopeful were glad to put their hands into those of the Shepherds and hold them very tightly indeed. The rock was just at the edge of the mountain, and when the little pilgrims looked down from it they could see a valley far below them, and upon the ground at the bottom of the valley lay the bodies of many dead people.

"Did they fall from this rock?" asked Hopeful.

"Yes," replied the Shepherds. "This is the Rock of Error, and pilgrims who leave the Way of the King, and wander upon the mountains alone, are fond of climbing up this pathway, because they think they will have a better view from the rock. But when they look over, the sight of the deep valley makes them giddy, and they fall and are killed."

Then the Shepherds took the children to another place, which was called Mount Caution. From it they looked upon a wide plain, where numbers of men, women, and children were walking up and down. But they walked in a strange way, stretching out their hands as if to feel what was before them, and Christian noticed that they kept stumbling upon the rocks.

"Are they blind?" he asked.

Experience answered that they were.

"Did you see a stile on the left-hand side of the road, not very far from these mountains?" asked Watchful.

"Yes," replied Christian.

"Beyond that stile is a path which leads to a strong castle. In the castle lives a giant named Despair. Many pilgrims go over into his meadow, because near to the stile the Way of the King is rough and stony, and the Giant's path looks green and smooth. Then they almost always lose their way, and Despair seizes them and carries them to his castle. He is very cruel to them, and at last, if he does not kill them, he puts out their eyes and brings them down to this plain, where they wander about until they die."

Christian and Hopeful looked at each other, but they did not speak. Perhaps, if they had not escaped from Doubting Castle by the help of the little key, they too would have been left to perish upon the plain!

The Shepherds now went down the mountains, on the side that was farthest from the Way of the King. Soon they came to a spot that reminded Christian of the entrance to the Dark Valley. Great black rocks hung over the path, and the children could see only a very little distance down the narrow road, because of the thick mist that lay before them.

"This is another dangerous place," said Knowledge, "and pilgrims who walk alone upon the mountains are often lost here. That path leads into the country of the Wicked Prince, and pilgrims who enter it are never able to find their way back again."

All these things made the little pilgrims very thoughtful. But Christian afterward said, "I am glad that we saw them, although I was frightened, because now we shall be very careful indeed about keeping in the Way of the King."

38

Ignorance

*L*ast of all the Shepherds brought the little pilgrims to the top of a hill called Mount Clear, from which they could see a very long way indeed. Far in the distance a beautiful light was shining, which dazzled their eyes when they tried to look at it.

"In the midst of that light," said a Shepherd, "is the Celestial City. If your eyes are strong you will be able to see its gates."

But the light was brighter than that of the sun at midday, and its glory was too great for human eyes to bear.

"I can only see it shining," said little Christian.

"It is too bright for you," said Sincere, "but we have a glass called Faith, which will make it seem clearer."

Christian took the glass, but the thought of the King's City, which he had so longed to see, made him tremble, and his hand shook so that he could not hold the glass steadily. Then Hopeful tried, but the tears came into his eyes.

"It dazzles me," he said, "but I think I can see something like a gate."

The walk upon the mountains had taken up the whole of the morning, so the Shepherds led the children back to the tents and made them rest a little while before they went away.

"When you have traveled a little farther," said Experience, "you will very likely meet a man called the Flatterer. He will try to lead you out of the Way of the King, but you must not listen to what he says."

Then Watchful told them that they would soon come to a place called the Enchanted Ground, where the air made the pilgrims feel very sleepy. "It was a part of the Wicked Prince's country, and if his servants find you sleeping there they will carry you away."

"We will give you this little map," said Knowledge, putting a sheet of paper into Christian's hand. "All the places you will have to pass are marked upon it, and if you look at it carefully, you cannot lose your way."

As Christian and Hopeful went down the mountain path they talked together of all that the Shepherds had shown them.

"If we could only have seen the Celestial City," said Christian, "I should have been so glad."

"Well," replied Hopeful, "we did see the glory of it, and we know that now it is not *very* far away."

At the foot of the mountain the boys came to the corner of a little crooked lane. This lane led from a country called Conceit, and a lad was running along toward the Way of the King when Christian and Hopeful passed.

"Where do you come from?" asked Christian, for the boy soon overtook them.

"From the country beyond the hills," he replied, "and I am going to the Celestial City."

"But do you think they will let you in?" said Christian.

"Why not? They let everybody else in."

"Not everybody. We have our Rolls to show. Did the King send you one?"

"No, but I don't suppose that will matter. I am His servant, because I always do what He bids me. I have heard that He wishes people to leave their own lands and travel to His city, so I am going, just as you are."

"But," said Christian, "the King's pilgrims ought to come in at the Wicket-gate and pass by the Cross. Then the Shining Ones bring them a white dress and a Roll. I am afraid you didn't know that."

"You needn't make such a fuss about it," replied the boy, whose name was Ignorance. "I don't know where you come from, but very likely you were living near to the Wicket-gate, and of course it was convenient for you to enter it. It is a *very* long way from my home, and nobody ever thinks of going to it. In fact, I don't believe that anybody knows the way! We have that pleasant green lane, which saves all trouble and makes our pilgrimage shorter."

Christian scarcely knew what to answer, and as Ignorance stopped to gather some fruit the little pilgrims passed on without him. He did not run after them, and Hopeful said, "Shall we wait for him?"

"I think not," replied Christian. "Perhaps he will join us presently."

39

The Story of Little Faith

Christian and Hopeful had not walked very far before they saw a band of soldiers in the distance. They were clothed in dark armor, which did not shine as Christian's did, and the little pilgrims knew that they belonged to the army of the Wicked Prince.

"Do you think they will hurt us?" said Hopeful.

"I don't know," replied Christian, and the boys both felt frightened, although they kept steadily on their way.

But as the soldiers drew nearer the children saw that they had a prisoner among them, and they knew by his dress that he was one of the King's pilgrims. The soldiers were hurrying him along, and they took no notice of Christian and Hopeful as they passed by. The pilgrim hung his head, for he was ashamed to let the children see his face.

He had once loved the King, and he had traveled very nearly to the gates of the Celestial City. Then he began to wander from the straight path, and before long he met with some servants of the Wicked Prince, who pretended to be very kind to him. He stayed with them, and soon he forgot the good King and left off obeying His laws. He allowed his bright armor to grow rusty, and his garments became soiled and ragged. His Roll was lost, and no one would have known that he had ever served the King at all.

But one day something reminded him of the Celestial City, and he began to feel sorry for what he had done and to wonder whether the King would forgive him. After a while he left his new friends and tried to find his way back again into the straight path. The Wicked Prince heard that he was gone and sent a band of soldiers to look for him. When the poor pilgrim drew his sword to defend himself he found that it was spoiled with rust and he could not use it. So the soldiers bound him with chains and were now taking him back into the country of the Wicked Prince.

Christian and Hopeful were glad that the soldiers did not speak to them, but they were also very sorry for the pilgrim, who seemed to be in great trouble.

"I remember," said Christian, as they went on, "when I was at the Palace Beautiful I read a story of a pilgrim named Little Faith, who was robbed not very far from this place. I think the Wicked Prince's servants often come here, and we must be very careful or they may perhaps hurt us."

"Tell me about Little Faith," said Hopeful. "How was he robbed?"

"He was very tired," replied Christian, "and he sat down upon the grass to rest, and fell asleep. It was just at the corner of one of the lanes that we have passed, so it was not a safe place to sleep in. Three bad boys (I think their names were Faint Heart, Mistrust, and Guilt) were playing in the lane, and they saw Little Faith lying at the corner, so they thought they would steal his things. He was just waking when they seized him, and before he had time to get his sword they threw him upon the ground and beat him dreadfully. Then they took all the money out of his pockets, and perhaps they would have killed him, but they thought they heard someone coming."

"Who was it?"

"There wasn't anyone really, but they knew they were doing wrong, and they were frightened. There is a little village called Good Confidence somewhere among these mountains, and Great Grace, one of the King's Captains, lives there. The boys thought he had seen them, and so they ran away."

"And what became of Little Faith? Was he hurt very much?"

"Yes, but they had not found his Roll, so, although he was grieved to lose his money, he felt comforted, and after a little while he was able to get up and go on his journey."

40

The Flatterer and His Net

*T*he boys were talking together about Little Faith and his troubles when they came to a place where a road led out of the Way of the King in such a manner that it was very difficult to see which path was the right one. If you stood on one side of the road, the right-hand path seemed to be straight; but if you crossed over to the other side, the left-hand path looked quite straight also.

"I don't know *which* is right!" said Christian, and they stood still to consider.

Now the Shepherds had given the children a little map, and if they had looked at it they would have seen at once which path to take. But instead of doing this, they began to waste their time by crossing the road from side to side, trying to find out for themselves which was the straightest of the two paths.

Presently a man came up behind them. His face was dark and ugly, but he wore a white robe, and the children supposed that he was a pilgrim.

"What is the matter?" he asked. "You seem to be very much puzzled."

"Oh," replied Christian, "we are going to the King's City, and we cannot make out which of these paths is the right one!"

The man laughed. "Is that all?" he said. "You need not look so troubled about it. I am going to the Celestial City myself. Follow me, and I will show you the way."

So, without waiting to be sure that the man was really a pilgrim, Christian and Hopeful followed him. But very soon they discovered their mistake, for instead of looking toward the Celestial City, they found that they were going back to the Delectable Mountains.

"This path is not straight, I am sure!" exclaimed Christian.

Hopeful stopped at once. "Don't you think it is?" he said, in a frightened voice.

"No. We ought to be looking the other way. See, there are the hills where we were walking this morning. This path is leading us back to them."

"That man has deceived us," said Hopeful.

"We must turn back again."

"But perhaps he will run after us and kill us. He cannot be a real pilgrim."

"I don't know," said Christian. "I wish we had not followed him! Let us run away."

The boys turned round hastily, but at that very moment the man turned also, and before they had time to take a single step toward the Way of the King they found themselves entangled in a large net, which he had thrown over them. They fell upon the ground, crying aloud for help, but the man only laughed and walked away. Then his white robe slipped from his shoulders, and they saw that he was a servant of the Wicked Prince and had dressed himself like a pilgrim in order to deceive anyone who would listen to him.

Christian and Hopeful struggled hard to free themselves from the dreadful net, but the more they pulled at it the tighter it became, and at last they were forced to lie still, crying together and thinking how foolish they had been.

"That man must be the Flatterer," said Christian, "and the Shepherds told us not to listen to him."

"Yes," said Hopeful, "and we never looked at the map which they gave us."

"We are very bad pilgrims," sobbed Christian. "We are always doing naughty things. If only the King will save us this once, I don't think we shall ever be so foolish again!"

41

The Little Pilgrims Are
Rescued by the Shining One

*T*he little pilgrims began to fear that they would have to spend the night beneath the net of the Flatterer. "And perhaps," said Christian, "he has gone to tell the Wicked Prince, and he will send his soldiers to carry us away."

Just when the sun was setting the children heard footsteps coming nearer and nearer, and even Hopeful could not help trembling. But only one man came in sight, and they knew by his shining garments and gentle face that he was really one of the King's true servants.

When he saw the little pilgrims he stopped. "How did you get into this net?" he asked.

"We were puzzled," said Christian, "and we could not make out which way to take. Then a man with a white robe came to us and told us he was going to the Celestial City, so we followed him."

"It was the Flatterer," said the King's servant, and then he stooped down and tore the net into pieces. Christian and Hopeful were soon able to creep out of it, and they stood upon the path before him, waiting until he should tell them what to do. His face was grave, and Christian remembered how Evangelist had looked at him in the same way when he found him wandering among the terrible rocks.

The Shining One turned toward the Way of the King and bade the boys come after him. Christian slipped his hand into Hopeful's, and they walked on together. When they were once more in the right path the Shining One stopped. "Where did you sleep last night?" he asked.

"With the Shepherds upon the mountains."

"Did they not give you a little map of the way?"

"Yes," said the boys, and they hung their heads, for they felt very much ashamed.

"Did you look at your map when you were puzzled?"

"No," whispered Hopeful, and Christian added, "We forgot."

"And what else did the Shepherds say to you? Did they warn you about the Flatterer?"

"They told us we were not to listen to him."

"And yet you *did* listen to him. How was that?"

"We did not think that man *could* be the Flatterer, because he spoke so kindly to us."

The tears were now running down the little pilgrims' cheeks, and the Shining One laid his hands upon their shoulders and spoke gently to them. "You have been very foolish," he said, "but I think you are sorry."

"We are very, very sorry," sobbed poor little Christian, "and it was more my fault than Hopeful's."

"No," said the Shining One, "you were both wrong. If the King had not sent me to look for you, you might have been killed or carried away by the soldiers of the Wicked Prince."

But although the King had sent His servant to seek for the lost children and to bring them back into the right path, He was not pleased with them, and He had commanded the Shining One to punish them for their foolishness.

"The King will forgive you," he said, "but I shall be obliged to punish you, because you have now been pilgrims for a long time, and you would not have lost your way if you had done as the Shepherds told you."

Then Christian and Hopeful saw that he held a little whip in his hand, and with this he struck them both many times. The strokes of the whip hurt them very much, but they knew that they deserved the punishment. When it was over, the Shining One told them that the King would not remember their naughtiness anymore.

"Our dear Prince," he said, "was once a pilgrim, and He has not forgotten the dangers and difficulties of the way. He is always watching over you, and when you are careless He begs His Father to forgive you for His sake."

42

Unbelief

*A*fter the Shining One had left them the little pilgrims went steadily on their way, and for two or three days they met with neither friends nor enemies. They were now crossing a very wide plain, which lay between the Delectable Mountains and a beautiful country with low hills and long valleys. This was marked upon their map as the "Land of Delight." Part of the plain was called the Enchanted Ground, and Hopeful reminded Christian that the Shepherds had warned them not to fall asleep there.

"I had not forgotten," said Christian, "but I am glad you remembered too. We must be very careful now, for after all this long journey it would be dreadful if we were carried away like that poor little pilgrim whom we saw the other day."

"We will not listen to any more Flatterers," said Hopeful. "Is there not a man upon the road before us now?"

"Yes," replied Christian, "and his face is turned away from the Celestial City. He must be coming to meet us."

"I don't think he is one of the Shining Ones," said Hopeful, as the man drew nearer. "No, he has pilgrim's dress, but he is walking the wrong way."

The man, whose name was Unbelief, stopped when he met the children and asked them where they were going. He had a pleasant face, and his voice was gentle, but the boys knew that they must not trust his words.

"We are going to the Celestial City, the city of the King," said Christian, in answer to his question.

Unbelief laughed. "You poor little fellows!" said he. "Have you really traveled all this long way without finding out the truth?"

"What truth?" asked Hopeful.

"It is such a tiresome journey," continued Unbelief, "and if you ever get to the end of it you will only be disappointed."

"Why?"

Then Unbelief pretended to look sad. "There is no King," he said, "and no Celestial City."

"Oh, but there *is*," exclaimed Christian. "We have heard about it from the King's own servants!"

Unbelief put his hand upon the boy's shoulder and tried to turn him around. "My dear child, you are quite young, and I am growing old. Listen to what I have to say. Long, long ago I heard the very same story which was told to you. I left my home and came to look for the King's City."

"Well," said Christian, "you will find it soon, will you not?"

"No," replied Unbelief. "I have been much farther than you have. I have spent twenty years as a pilgrim, and I can find no city at all."

Then Christian turned to Hopeful with a very sorrowful face. "Oh, do you think he is speaking the truth?"

"No," said Hopeful. "I am sure he is not. Do not listen to him! You know we *saw* the city from the Delectable Mountains. Let us make haste, or the Shining One will have to punish us again."

Unbelief stood by, watching the two boys. "Come back with me," he said, "and I will take you safely to your own homes again."

But Christian answered him bravely. "You are trying to deceive us, but we do not believe what you say. We are quite sure that the King's word is true, and that there *is* a Celestial City. We saw its gates when we were with the Shepherds."

Unbelief shook his head. "You are mistaken, but you can go and look for it. I am going back to my own country."

"And we are going to the King," replied Christian.

So they went on again, and Unbelief laughed at them as he turned away.

43

The Enchanted Ground

*T*hey came, a little later in the day, to that part of the plain that was called the Enchanted Ground. It was a very pleasant place, so sheltered by the hills that the air was always soft and warm. The streams flowed gently along, the breeze scarcely stirred the leaves of the trees, and everything around seemed quite happy. But the meadows on either side of the Way of the King were not fenced in like those in the beautiful Valley of Peace, therefore it was not safe for pilgrims to lie down and rest in them. The servants of the Wicked Prince were often hidden among the rocks and bushes, and when travelers were foolish enough to sleep there they were almost sure to be robbed, if they were not carried away altogether.

"Oh, dear," exclaimed Hopeful presently, "I am *so* sleepy! My eyes keep shutting every minute. Do let us sit down and rest for a while."

"Not here!" said Christian, and he seized Hopeful's arm and shook him gently. "Hopeful! Hopeful! You are forgetting! This is the Enchanted Ground!"

"Well," replied Hopeful drowsily, "there is no one to hurt us. I will only stay a few minutes, Christian. Don't wait for me."

He threw himself down upon the grass, but Christian quickly pulled him up again, and this time he shook him violently.

"What *are* you thinking about?" he said. "Don't you remember what the Shepherd told us?" And he did not rest until Hopeful was thoroughly awakened.

Then the little pilgrim was frightened at the thought of his danger. *What should I have done if I had been alone! I am sure I should have fallen asleep. I have never felt so tired in all my life.*

"I was just beginning to feel sleepy too," Christian told Hopeful, "but shaking you roused me up. We may be very thankful that we were together. Let us talk about something interesting. That will keep us awake. You have never told me how it was that you began to be a pilgrim."

"I started before you did," said Hopeful. "I knew Faithful very well, and when first Evangelist talked to him he used to come to me afterward and tell me what he had heard about the King. I did not care much then, but after a time I thought it would be nice to live in the Celestial City, so one day I ran off to the Wicket-gate and began my journey. But when I came to Vanity Fair I stopped to play with the boys in the streets, and at last they persuaded me not to go any farther, so I stayed there."

"You didn't like it really, did you?"

"No. At least, I liked it sometimes, but I used often to feel frightened and unhappy. When pilgrims passed through the town I was ashamed and afraid lest they should see me. Then you came with Faithful, and the minute I saw him I knew who he was."

"Did you see us beaten?" asked Christian.

"Yes, and I watched you when you were in the cage. Once I crept close up to the bars. I think you must have been asleep, but Faithful saw me, and he spoke to me."

"What did he say?"

"He begged me to leave the city at once, and he said the King would forgive me for our dear Prince's sake. Then I saw all that dreadful sight, and I knew that Faithful had suffered patiently because he loved the King, and I made up my mind that, when you were set free, I would ask you to let me go with you."

"I am so glad you did," said Christian. "We have been very happy together. Don't you feel glad too?"

"Yes," replied Hopeful, "indeed I do! I am sure now that the King loves me, and it will not be very long before we are both safe in His beautiful city."

44

The Little Pilgrims
Wait for Ignorance

*A*ll this time Ignorance had been traveling slowly along by himself. The Flatterer and Unbelief never took any notice of him. They knew he had not begun his pilgrimage in the right way and that when he reached the Celestial City the King's servants would not allow him to enter its gates but would send him back to his own master, the Wicked Prince. So Ignorance met with no trouble or difficulty and did not even feel sleepy when he crossed the Enchanted Ground.

While Hopeful and little Christian were passing over that dangerous plain they remembered Ignorance and wondered how he was getting on. Presently Hopeful looked back.

"He is only a little way behind us," said he. "Shall we wait for him?"

"Perhaps it would be better," replied Christian. "Then, if he feels sleepy, we can keep him awake."

The little pilgrims waited, but although Ignorance saw that they were standing still, he did not seem to care about overtaking them.

"It is a pity for you to stay behind," said Christian, as the lad came slowly toward him. "Won't you walk with us?"

"I don't care," replied Ignorance. "I would just as soon walk by myself. I have always so much to think about."

"What is it that you think of?" asked Hopeful.

"The King and the Celestial City."

"But *thinking* about them is not enough," said Christian. "We ought to be very anxious to *see* the King and His City."

"So I am."

"Then why don't you travel faster?"

"I am traveling quite fast enough. I am sure that I shall reach the City some day, and why should I not take my journey comfortably?"

"But, perhaps, if you are so careless about it, you will fall into trouble or danger."

"Well, if I do the King will help me."

"The King will not help you if you do not try to obey Him," said Hopeful, who felt sure that Ignorance did not really know much about the King and His laws.

"I *do* try to obey Him," answered the boy. "I have left my home and become a pilgrim. What else can I do?"

"You did not pass by the Cross," said Christian. "And I am afraid that, if you have not a Roll and a pilgrim's dress, the King's servant will not let you enter the City."

"I am sure you are quite wrong in what you say," replied Ignorance. "I have read that the Prince will give a white robe to every pilgrim, and no doubt He will send me mine soon. Why should I travel to the Wicket-gate and the Cross to look for it? It would seem as if I did not believe what the Prince had said!"

Then Christian remembered the paper that Evangelist had given to him before he left home. Perhaps Ignorance had had one like it. "Did the King send you a message?" he asked.

"A message? No, of course He did not! I should never expect a great King to send a message to a boy like me."

Poor little Christian felt quite puzzled. "I don't know what to say to him," he whispered to Hopeful. "I am sure he is wrong, but he will not believe us."

But Ignorance was now tired of talking. "I really can't keep up with you," he said. "You must go on by yourselves." And as the little pilgrims did not know what else they could say to him, they went on and left him to follow as slowly as he wished.

45

The Land of Delight

*T*he little pilgrims, having passed over the Enchanted Ground, found themselves in the Land of Delight. It was the most beautiful country they had ever seen. Its mountains were covered with trees, and its valleys were green with soft grass and gay with the loveliest flowers. In the distance shone the glorious light that the Shepherds had shown them from the Delectable Mountains, and as the children's eyes grew accustomed to its brightness they were able to distinguish the walls and gates of the Celestial City.

The Wicked Prince and his soldiers never came into the Land of Delight. The people who lived there were all true servants of the King, and they received Christian and Hopeful very kindly.

"Your troubles are over now," they said. "You have only to stay here and be happy until the King sends for you."

"Will He send soon?" asked Christian.

"We cannot tell you that," replied the people. "Sometimes the pilgrims live quietly in this land for many years, and sometimes the King gives them work to do for Him in the country of the Wicked Prince, but at last they all go to the Celestial City to dwell forever in His presence."

"I remember," said Christian, "when Help drew me out of the Slough, he said that he had been to the gates of the City, but the King had given him some work which he would have to do before he entered it."

And while he wandered up and down the mountains and along the beautiful valleys with Hopeful, little Christian began to wonder whether his mother was living in this Land of Delight, or whether she had gone into the City. He looked anxiously at the people whom he met, but he did not see anyone whose face was like his mother's picture. "The King must have sent for her," he said. "Oh, will it not be nice to see her again! Perhaps she has heard that we are here, and she may be watching for us even now."

The little pilgrims spent many happy days in the Land of Delight, and one morning they came to a valley that was laid out in vineyards and large gardens. The gates were all wide open, and as the boys stopped to look at the trees and flowers one of the gardeners spoke to them.

"You need not stay outside," he said. "These are the King's gardens, and they are for the pilgrims to walk in."

Then he took their hands and led them about among the vines and flowers, and in the evening he showed them a quiet little arbor where they might lie down and sleep safely.

"Oh," said Christian, as they sat watching the sun, which was slowly sinking behind the hills, "don't you feel glad that we came? I seem to be forgetting all the troubles we have had, now that we are so happy."

"I am so thankful that I ran away from Vanity Fair," said Hopeful, "and it was such a good thing that I did not lose my Roll there. I don't know how it was that I managed to keep it safely!"

"And now we have only to wait for the King's message," continued Christian. "I would go away and work if He wished it, but I think I would like best to go straight into the City."

"So would I," said Hopeful, and then they lay down side by side, as they had done in the Valley of Peace, and slept quietly until the morning.

46

The Dark River

*T*he Land of Delight was so very near to the Celestial City that the Shining Ones often came down to visit the people who lived there. Their faces shone with a beautiful light, as the face of Christian's mother had done when he saw her in his dream, and their garments were all white and glistening. Very often they brought messages from the King to His servants, and the little pilgrims knew that some day a message would be given to them.

I told you that they slept one night in the King's garden, and the next morning when they were walking slowly along among the vines, they saw two of the Shining Ones coming down the path to meet them.

"You are traveling to the Celestial City?" they asked.

"Yes," replied the children.

Then the Shining Ones asked many questions and desired both Christian and Hopeful to tell them of all that had happened since they began their pilgrimage. Christian told of all his difficulties and dangers, and Hopeful told how he had wasted his time in Vanity Fair.

"We have often behaved badly," they said, "but we are really sorry, and we do love the King with all our hearts."

"He knows that you do," replied the Shining Ones, "and He has forgiven you for all your mistakes and disobedience for the sake of His dear Son. He has sent us now to tell you that He wishes you to enter into His City."

When Hopeful heard this his heart was full of joy. Little Christian was glad also, but when he thought of going into the presence of the King he began to feel timid, and he said to the Shining Ones, "Will you go with us?"

"We will go a little way with you," they said, "and we will meet you again at the gates of the City."

Then they desired the children to follow them, and they all went out of the garden and down to the shore of a very wide river. Its waters were dark and rough, but the light from the Celestial City was shining brightly beyond it.

"Oh," cried Christian, "how are we to cross over?"

"You will have to walk through the water," replied the Shining Ones, "but you must not be afraid. The City is on the other side, and you will very soon be safe within its gates."

Hopeful raised his head and looked across the river, and on the opposite shore he could see the pathway winding up the hillside towards the glorious golden gates. "Oh, Christian!" he said, "we need not be frightened now! We are so *very* near to the City."

But little Christian's eyes had grown dim with fear, and he could not see the light beyond the river. He shivered as he looked at the water, and then he turned once more to the Shining Ones. "It is deep!" he said. "We shall drown if we try to cross it!"

"No," replied the Shining Ones, "you will not find it too deep. You must not look at the water—you must lift up your eyes to the light, and the King will help you."

"Will you come with us?" asked Christian again, and Hopeful wondered why he looked so pale and frightened.

"We cannot come with you," replied the Shining Ones, "but we shall meet you on the other side and lead you into the presence of the King."

"Did my mother cross it safely?"

"Yes, and she is waiting for you and longing to see you. Do not be afraid! Trust in the King, and remember all that He has done for you."

Then the Shining Ones turned away, and Hopeful put his arm around his little companion's shoulders. "Come, Christian," he said, "this is our very last trouble, and it will soon be over. Let us go together, and I am sure the King will take care of us."

So the little pilgrims went slowly down the bank and stepped into the water.

47

Ignorance Crosses the River

*W*hen Ignorance entered the Land of Delight the people who met him spoke kindly to him, as they had done to Christian and Hopeful. But they soon found out that he was not a true pilgrim and that he did not care to talk with them, so they left him to himself. He passed by the gates of the King's gardens, but the gardeners did not invite him to come in. And the Shining Ones, although they often watched him as he walked along, did not speak to him or give him any gracious message from the King!

At last he came to the brink of the Dark River. He could see the walls of the Celestial City on the other side, and he knew that his journey would not be ended until he had crossed the water. He stood for a few minutes wondering what he should do, and then he lay down on the grass.

I will rest a little, he thought, *and perhaps someone else will be coming presently. I do not see any bridge, so there must be a boat to carry the pilgrims over.*

There was a boat, but it belonged to the Wicked Prince, and the King's pilgrims never used it. The boatman, whose name was Vain-Hope, soon saw Ignorance lying upon the bank and rowed toward him.

"It is time for you to go over the river," he said. "I have brought my boat for you."

Ignorance was pleased, and he got up at once, saying, "I suppose the King sent you."

"Yes," replied the man. "The water is not very deep in some places, and many pilgrims try to walk through it. But there is no need to do so, because I am always ready to take them over."

He held out his hand, and Ignorance took it and stepped down into the boat. Then Vain-Hope caught up his oars and rowed quickly across the rough water.

"What shall I do now?" asked Ignorance, when he had climbed up the opposite bank.

Vain-Hope pointed to a little winding path. "That is the best way," he said. "It is smooth and easy. If the Shining Ones had come to meet you, they would have taken you by another road, which is steep and difficult to climb. Go straight up to the gate, and you will soon find your way to the King's palace."

He pushed his boat off from the shore, and Ignorance turned round and began to climb the hill toward the City. He did not meet anyone, and when he reached the gates he found that they were closed. He looked up and saw some words written upon the archway in letters of gold—

"BLESSED ARE THEY THAT DO HIS COMMANDMENTS."

Well, thought Ignorance, *I* have *obeyed the King always,* and he knocked at the gate. He quite forgot that the King had desired His pilgrims to begin their journey at the Wicket-gate and to travel by the Way of the Cross. He had heard of this many times, but he had not cared about it, and so the King's blessing could not be given him. He knocked twice, but no one opened the gates. Presently one of the King's servants came to the top of the archway, and when he saw Ignorance he said, "Where do you come from, and why are you knocking at the King's gate?"

"I am a pilgrim," replied the boy. "I have just crossed the river, and I wish to live in the Celestial City."

"I will take your Roll," said the King's servant, "and carry it to my Master."

Ignorance knew that he had never received a Roll, but he put his hand into the folds of his clothes and pretended to feel for it. The King's servant waited a little while, but at last he said, "I am afraid you have come without one." Then he went down from the gate to ask the King what he should do.

Poor Ignorance stood outside, and now he began to wish that he had not been so careless about his journey. *The city is so beautiful,* he thought. *I should like to have lived here always, and I am afraid they will not let me go in!*

When the King heard that a pilgrim had come to the gate who had neither a white robe nor a Roll, He said, "I do not know him. He must be sent away."

Then two of the Shining Ones came quickly and bound the hands and feet of the foolish boy and carried him away from the Celestial City into the country of the Wicked Prince. His cruel master rejoiced when he was brought back and took care that he should never again have a chance of escaping.

"It was your own fault," he said, when he found Ignorance crying bitterly at the thought of his lost happiness. "If you had really wished to live with the King, you should have done exactly as He told you."

W.L.C.

48

The End of the Pilgrimage

*L*ittle Christian clasped his hands together as he felt the cold waters of the Dark River rushing round his body. Hopeful kept close to him and tried to hold him up, but the little pilgrim soon lost his footing and cried out, "I am sinking! The water is all going over me!"

"No, it is only rough," said Hopeful. "Do not be so frightened. I can feel the ground at the bottom of the river, and it is quite firm. We shall cross safely, and then we shall have no more trouble."

"Perhaps you will cross," whispered Christian faintly, "but I am sure I cannot. I shall never see the King, and I did *so* wish to live with Him always!"

"You *will* live with Him. Look up, Christian, and don't think about the water. We can see everything quite clearly now. The City is full of light, and the Shining Ones are waiting for us at the gates."

"They are waiting for you," said Christian, "not for me," and then his head sank down on Hopeful's shoulders. For a little while he did not seem to hear anything that his companion said. But Hopeful held him tightly in his arms and prayed very earnestly to the King to help them both in this last trouble.

Presently little Christian opened his eyes, and as the light from the Celestial City fell upon his face he cried out suddenly, "Oh, I can see it all now! It shines like the sun, and I heard the voice of the Prince. He said, 'I will be with you in the waters.' "

"Then I am sure we need not be frightened," said Hopeful. "Take hold of my hand again. The Prince will never break His promise."

So little Christian's courage came back to him, and he did not faint or tremble anymore. Hand in hand the little pilgrims made their way across the Dark River, and after a time its bed seemed to grow firmer, and its waters were less rough. Then they saw that the two Shining Ones who had brought them down to the river were waiting to receive them. In a few moments the dreadful passage was over. Gentle hands drew them out of the water, and they stood safely upon the shore.

The Celestial City was built upon a hill, and a broad, straight road led from the river to its gates. This road was steep, as Vain-Hope had said when he pointed out the little winding path that Ignorance had taken. But Christian and Hopeful did not find it difficult, for the Shining Ones held their hands and took care that they did not slip.

"We shall soon be in the City now," said Christian, who had forgotten all his fear and sorrow and could only look up at the bright walls and gates that rose before him.

"Yes," replied the Shining One with whom he was walking, "you will see the King in His beauty, and He will receive you as His own child."

"Will He really let me live in His City always?"

"Yes, and you will never be tired or sad anymore. You will have work to do for the King, but it will be easy and pleasant, and you will love to do it."

"Shall I find my mother?" said Christian; for in the midst of his happiness he remembered her and longed for the time when he should see her.

"She is coming to meet you," said the Shining One. "She knows that you are with us, and she is so glad that your pilgrimage is over and that you have crossed the river safely."

49

The Celestial City

The little pilgrims were now very near to the City, and a band of the King's servants, who had been watching at the gate, came quickly down the steep path to meet them.

"These are two of the King's little pilgrims," said the Shining Ones, "and we are bringing them home to the Celestial City."

Then, as Christian looked up, one face seemed to him to be brighter than all the rest. His mother was standing before him, and her eyes shone as she watched him.

"Is it my little Christian?" she asked, and the Shining Ones made way for her. But little Christian knew her in a moment, and he ran into her arms.

"I have come to you, Mother, I have come!" he cried. "The King has taken care of me, and some day He will bring my father too."

"I shall never lose you again," she said. "The King is very good. Come with me into His city that we may thank Him together."

Oh, how happy little Christian felt when he put his hand in his mother's and knew that she would never be taken away from him again! And although Hopeful had not any friends to welcome him, for he had left them all behind him in the City of Destruction, the Shining Ones gathered round and spoke so kindly to him that he was comforted and forgot his loneliness.

Little Christian had left his armor on the other side of the river, for he would never need to fight again, and now he looked down anxiously at his clothes. He had tried to take care of them, but he knew that they had become soiled and dusty during his long journey, and he feared that the King would be displeased when He saw them. But the waters of the Dark River had washed away all the dust and stains. Even Hopeful, whose clothes had been sadly spoiled while he stayed in Vanity Fair, found that his dress looked as fresh and new as it did when he first received it.

Close to the walls of the Celestial City a number of men were standing, with silver trumpets in their hands. When Christian and Hopeful came up to them, they blew their trumpets loudly to let the people in the City know that some pilgrims were waiting to enter into the King's presence. Then the Shining Ones told the children to knock at the gate, and the King's servant looked down from the archway and took the Rolls, which they gave to him, and carried them to the Palace. The Rolls were sealed with the Prince's own seal, and when the King saw it He was glad and desired His servant to open the gates at once and to bring the little pilgrims before Him.

The people of the City had heard the sound of the silver trumpets, and they all knew what it meant. When Christian and Hopeful passed through the gateway, they found a great company waiting to receive them with sweet music and songs of welcome. Everyone looked glad and happy, for there was no sorrow in the Celestial City, and no weariness, and no pain.

At first the children's eyes were dazzled by the golden light that shone around them, but by degrees they grew accustomed to it and were able to look up. Before them, in the middle of the City, rose a very stately palace, far more glorious than the Palace Beautiful.

"Does the King live there?" whispered Christian to his mother, for his hand was still clasped in hers.

"Yes," she replied, "and when you have knelt before Him and seen His glory, you will be perfectly happy forever."

"I am happy *now*," said little Christian, "because I have found you, and you love me."

"Ah, yes," she answered, "but the love of the King is far greater than mine!"

The little pilgrims had now reached the threshold of the Palace, and as the doors were thrown open they heard a sound of the very sweetest music. The Prince Himself was waiting to receive them, and He smiled upon them and took their hands in His own. Then He led them into the Palace, and the whole City was filled with joy because their pilgrimage was over and they had been brought safely through the Dark River into the presence of the King.

PART 2

CHRISTIANA

50

A Letter from the King

*C*hristiana had always loved little Christian, and when the other children told her that he had run away from them across the plain, and that they believed he had really gone to the Celestial City, she was very sorry indeed.

She had often heard about the City. Her own father and mother were both living there. And while they were traveling upon the Way of the King, they had sent many loving messages to Christiana, desiring her to begin her pilgrimage and to bring her brothers and her little sister with her. But not very long before little Christian went away, she was told that her father had crossed the Dark River, and in a few days her mother followed him. Then Christiana received no more messages, and she felt sad and lonely.

When little Christian talked to her about his Book, she listened to him, but she did not believe what he said. "If my father and mother were really living in a beautiful city like that," she used to say, "I am sure they would not forget us. They would have sent me another message. I think they were lost in the Dark River, and we shall never see them anymore."

So when little Christian went away she feared that he would be lost too, and she could not help crying to think of it.

The summer and autumn passed, and the winter also. Then the spring came round again, and Christiana took her little sister, Innocence, into the fields to gather daisies. Innocence could run about now, and Christiana loved to see her playing happily among the flowers.

Last year, she thought, *Christian came with us into this very field the day before he went away, and we made daisy chains together. I wonder if he has found the Celestial City or whether he has been lost.*

She looked across the plain, and she could see the light in the distance, shining brightly above the Wicket-gate. "Perhaps," she said to herself, "I will go some day, but I must wait until Innocence is a little older. And I could not leave the boys by themselves. I am sure they would not go with me now." Then she lifted Innocence in her arms and turned back toward the City of Destruction.

In the evening, when she had put little Innocence to bed and the house was quite still, for the boys were playing in the market with their school-fellows, she sat down by the fire and thought of her father and mother, and of Christian also, and wished very much that she could see them all once more.

That night she had a strange dream. She fancied she had really found the Celestial City and that she was walking along its streets with little Christian. Innocence was there too, and the three boys, and they all went together into a beautiful palace, where the King Himself met them and spoke very graciously to them.

I wish it had been true and not a dream! she thought when she awoke. And as she could not go to sleep again she got up, although it was very early, and began to put the house in order. Presently she heard a knock at the door and cried, "Come in!"

She expected to see a neighbor, but when the door opened one of the strangers entered. Her name was Wisdom, and she was the daughter of Evangelist. Christiana knew her, for she had seen her in the city and had sometimes watched her gathering the children round her that she might talk to them about the King.

"I have been wishing to speak to you," she said, "but I have not been able to find you in the streets lately."

"No," replied Christiana, "I was tired of the streets, and I took my little sister into the fields."

Wisdom laid her hand gently upon the girl's shoulder. "I don't think you are very happy, Christiana."

"I am lonely," she answered.

"You have your three brothers, and Innocence."

"Yes, but I am lonely," she repeated. "My father and mother are gone, and little Christian, and I do not know what has become of them."

"They are with the King, in His glorious City."

"Ah!" said Christiana, "I have been told so often that the stories about the King and the Celestial City are not true."

"They are quite true," replied Wisdom. "The King is sorry that you do not believe them, and He has sent me to tell you that He wishes you to begin your pilgrimage at once and to bring the boys and Innocence with you."

"So many of us?" exclaimed Christiana.

"Yes. The King's City is large, and there is room in it for every pilgrim who comes to its gates. Do you not know how pleased your dear ones will be when they hear that those gates have been opened for you?"

The tears came into Christiana's eyes, but she wiped them away. "I will think about it," she said.

"This will help you," answered Wisdom, and she drew out a folded paper like that which Evangelist had given to Christian. "It is a letter from the King. Keep it safely and read it often, and when you reach the Celestial City you must show it to the Shining Ones who will meet you at the gate."

51

Christiana Shows
the Letter to Her Brothers

*C*hristiana could scarcely believe that the letter was really from the King, and for her. And when she had read it her heart was filled with joy and sorrow together—joy that the King should send her such a gracious message, and sorrow that she had not learned to love and obey Him before.

She looked up again at Wisdom, who was standing near her. "I will go," she said, "and I will try to take the children with me."

Wisdom smiled at her. "That is right," she said. "Do not wait any longer. The way is easier for children than for older people, and the King will help you in all your difficulties."

"Can you not go with us?" said Christiana. "Then I should not be frightened."

"No, I have other work to do. But you need not be frightened. You know the way to the Wicket-gate, and when you have passed through it, you will meet with many of the King's servants, who will be very kind to you."

Christiana read the King's letter many times over that day, and in the evening she showed it to Matthew, her eldest brother. "What shall I do?" she asked him.

"You will go—will you not?"

"I should like to go, and I would take Innocence. But what will become of you boys if I leave you alone?"

"We must go too," said Matthew. "At any rate *I* will."

"Will you really? Oh, I am so glad!"

"I have often thought about it," continued Matthew, "since we knew that our father and mother had crossed the Dark River. And when little Christian and Faithful went away, I was half inclined to follow them. It will be nice now for us all to go together."

Christiana smiled as she looked into the fire. "Mother would be so pleased to see us! But I do not know whether James and Joseph will come. Perhaps they will be afraid of the long journey."

Just at that moment the door opened, and the two younger boys ran in. "Oh!" exclaimed James, "we are *so* tired! What are you talking about, you two?"

"Christiana has had a letter," replied Matthew, and he laid the paper on the table, where his brothers could read it as they stood side by side.

"It is from the King!" said Joseph. "Why has He written to Christiana?"

"Who brought it?" asked James. "Do you think it *really* came from the King?"

"One of the strangers brought it. Her name is Wisdom. You have often seen her in the streets."

"I know her. She spoke to me one day, and I liked her. Shall you go?" Joseph came round to the fire and leaned against his sister's chair, looking into her face.

"Will you come with me?"

"I don't mind. Shall we have to fight anybody? And will there be any wild beasts?"

"I do not know, but Wisdom said we need not be frightened. The King will take care of us."

"I should like to be a pilgrim," said James, "but Innocence is so tiny, and you can't leave *her* behind."

"No," said Matthew, "of course not. She can walk a little, and we must carry her when she is tired."

"When shall we go?" asked Joseph. "We have to pass through that gate with the lamp over it, haven't we? Oh, don't you remember? Pliable went with little Christian last spring, and they fell into the Slough."

"We will be careful," said Matthew. "When can you be ready, Christiana? Tomorrow, or the next day?"

"The next day, I think. We can prepare everything at night, and then start very early, as soon as the gates of the city are opened."

52

The Children Leave
the City of Destruction

*I*n the afternoon of Christiana's last day in the City of Destruction, three or four girls who had been her friends ran in to see her.

"Oh, you *do* look busy!" cried one. "We came to ask you to go with us into the country tomorrow."

"I don't think I can," replied Christiana.

"Why, you are putting everything away!" exclaimed another. "You might be getting ready for a journey."

Christiana had not meant to say anything about the King's letter, but now she felt that it would be better to tell her friends what she intended to do.

"I have had a message from the King," she said, "and I am going to the Celestial City."

"Oh," cried the girls, "how *can* you be so foolish!"

"I am not foolish. I wish you would all come with me."

"And leave our beautiful city and all our friends! What will your poor little sister do, and the boys? It is very wrong of you, Christiana, to think of leaving them."

"They are going with me."

Then the girls laughed. "You must be mad! How can a baby like Innocence be a pilgrim? Just think of all we have heard about little Christian and his troubles. He was nearly lost in the Slough to begin with, and you know when Mistrust and Timorous came back they told us that he had met with lions on the Hill Difficulty."

"Yes," said another, "and you cannot have forgotten the news we had from Vanity Fair about the death of Faithful. You are a silly girl to run into such danger, especially when you have a baby sister and three brothers to take care of."

"Matthew is old enough now to take care of me," replied Christiana, "and we are not afraid. The King has promised to watch over us. Here is His letter. You can read it if you like."

But the girls did not believe in the King or care about His messages. "It is of no use wasting our time," they said. "You must do as you please, but you will soon wish yourself back again."

Christiana was not sorry when the door closed and she was once more alone. "I am glad Wisdom came to me," she said to herself, "for I should have thought just as they do if she had not spoken to me."

Matthew did not stay long in the city that day, and even James and Joseph were eager to begin their pilgrimage and came home early so that they might help Christiana.

"I have washed your clothes and mended them," she said, "but I never noticed before how shabby they were getting. You must keep them as tidy as you can, and perhaps the King will send us some new ones."

Very early in the morning the children went quietly away from their cottage and passed out at the gate of the city. The keeper did not stop them, for he thought they were only going to spend a long day in the meadows. Christiana carried Innocence in her arms, and Matthew had brought a bag with some food. James and Joseph ran on before them, for they were anxious to reach the Wicket-gate.

"Perhaps we may meet a lion," said Joseph, "but I shall not be frightened."

"Oh, no!" said James. "Pilgrims are always brave, and, of course, we must fight for our sisters."

Innocence clapped her tiny hands when she saw the daisies nodding their pretty white heads in the grass, and Matthew began to gather a few of them for her to carry with her. While he was doing this a little girl came in sight, running across the meadow from the city.

"Stop!" she cried. "Please let me speak to Christiana."

Christiana looked round. "It is Mercy," she said.

Mercy was out of breath with running, but she caught Christiana's hand and held it fast. "I didn't care to go with the other girls," she said. "May I walk a little way with you?"

"Oh, yes!" replied Christiana. "Why will you not go all the way?"

"I have had no message," said Mercy, for she had come into the cottage with her school-fellows and had seen the King's letter.

"That will not matter," said Matthew. "I am sure I have heard Evangelist say that the King would like *all* the children to become pilgrims."

But Mercy was timid, and she feared that the King might not receive her if she came to His City without being sent for.

"I will tell you what to do," said Christiana. "Come with us as far as the Wicket-gate, and we will ask the King's servant whether you may pass through."

Mercy was willing to do this, and as she was a gentle little girl and a favorite with the boys, they were glad to have her with them, and they all went on together very happily until they reached the Slough of Despond.

"This is where Pliable and little Christian were nearly smothered," said Christiana. "I do not know how we shall cross, for it seems very dangerous indeed."

The soft green mud was oozing between the tufts of grass, but as they looked carefully round, the children caught sight of the stepping-stones. James and Joseph skipped lightly from stone to stone. But Matthew held Mercy's hand, for she was afraid of falling, and Innocence clasped her little arms tightly round Christiana's neck. Soon they found themselves once more on firm ground, and they knew that no other unsafe place lay between the city and the Wicket-gate.

"We will walk quickly," said Christiana, "while the day is cool and pleasant, and perhaps we may be allowed to rest a little when we have entered the Way of the King."

53

At the Wicket-gate

*A*bout the middle of the day the six little pilgrims came up to the Wicket-gate.

"You are the eldest," said Matthew to Christiana, "and the King's letter was for you, so you had better knock, and tell the keeper why we have come."

Christiana knocked at the gate several times, but no one answered. Then a dog began to bark very furiously indeed, and although James and Joseph had promised to be brave, they both turned pale and whispered to Mercy, "Shall we go home again?"

"Oh, no!" said Mercy, but she felt frightened also.

"We must knock again," said Matthew. So Christiana lifted the knocker and rapped once more as loudly as she could.

Then Goodwill, who kept the gate, came out of his cottage and asked, "Who is there?" and when the dog heard his voice it left off barking.

"Please do not be vexed with us," said Christiana, "because we knocked so often. We thought you did not hear us, and we were frightened at the dog."

Goodwill was not vexed. He looked kindly at the children and asked, "Where do you come from? And what do you wish me to do for you?"

"We have come from the city where little Christian lived, and we are going to be the King's pilgrims if you will let us pass through the gate. These are my brothers, and this is my little sister."

Then Goodwill took Christiana's hand and led her through the gateway, saying, "Suffer the little children to come unto me, and forbid them not, for of such is the kingdom of heaven."

Christiana knew that these words had been spoken by the Prince Himself. She had seen them written in the old Book of which little Christian had been so fond, and she felt very happy as she entered the Way of the King with Innocence in her arms and her brothers by her side.

Poor little Mercy had not dared to follow her friends. She drew back when the gate was opened, and Goodwill did not see her. Then, as she heard the gate close and found herself alone, she began to cry, for she thought that perhaps Christiana would forget her. But Christiana had not forgotten her.

"We have a little girl with us," she said to Goodwill, "who wishes to go to the Celestial City. The King has not sent her a letter, so she is afraid—"

Christiana had not time to say anything more, for Mercy had grown frightened and was knocking upon the gate with all her might.

"Who is that?" said Goodwill, and Christiana answered that it must be Mercy, of whom she had just been speaking. So Goodwill opened the gate again and looked out.

Little Mercy was not strong, and the fear of being left behind had made her feel sick and faint. After knocking at the gate she had fallen upon the grass and could not even look up when she heard the voice of Goodwill.

The kind old man stooped down and lifted the child in his arms. "Do not be frightened," he said, and then Mercy opened her eyes. "Tell me why you have come."

"Oh," said Mercy, "I had no letter! It was only Christiana who asked me."

"Did she wish you to go to the Celestial City with her?"

"Yes, and I should like to go. Will the King be angry, or will He let me be a pilgrim?"

"The King's gate is open to everyone who knocks at it," said Goodwill. "Come in with me, little one, and do not cry or tremble anymore."

Then he led Mercy also through the gateway, and he gave her some sweet-scented herbs to smell, so that she did not feel faint anymore.

54

The Beginning of the Pilgrimage

"You must rest in my cottage for a little while," said Goodwill. He brought the children into a cool, quiet room, where he desired them to stay until he came for them.

"Oh," exclaimed Christiana, when they were left alone, "how glad I am that we are here!"

"I think *I* ought to be more glad than any of you," said Mercy.

"I was so afraid," continued Christiana, "when we knocked and nobody answered us. I thought perhaps we had had our long walk for nothing, especially when that dog barked so dreadfully."

"The worst time was when you were all gone, and I was left behind," said Mercy. "I didn't like to knock again, until I looked up and saw the words carved over the gateway. Then I knocked as hard as I could."

Christiana smiled. "You *did* knock!" she said. "I thought you meant to force the gate open."

"Well," said Mercy, "I couldn't help it. The gate was shut, and that fierce dog must have been somewhere near. *You* would have knocked loudly if you had felt so frightened! Was Goodwill angry? What did he say?"

"He was smiling. I don't think he was angry. But I wonder why he keeps that dog! If I had known about it, I am not sure whether I should have dared to come. However, we are safe now, and I am very glad indeed."

"So am I," said Mercy. "I think I will ask Goodwill why he allows such a savage dog to be near the gate."

"Yes," said James, "do ask him, Mercy! We are afraid it will bite us when we go away."

So when Goodwill returned, Mercy asked him why he kept the dog.

"It is not mine," he answered. "There is a great castle not far from this gate, which belongs to the Wicked Prince. The dog lives at the castle, but he can run along his master's ground until he comes close to my cottage. Then, when he hears the pilgrims knocking, he begins to bark. The Wicked Prince has taught him to do this, and once or twice he has broken through the fence and has bitten a pilgrim. But I always open the gate as quickly as possible, and you know the King's servants must not be frightened when danger is near to them."

He laid his hand gently on Mercy's head, and the little girl looked up at him. "It was wrong of me," she said. "Another time I will remember and trust the King to take care of me."

Then Christiana began to ask Goodwill about the Way of the King, and he was ready to answer all her questions. Afterwards, he told the little pilgrims to wash themselves, while he prepared a comfortable meal for them, so that they felt rested and refreshed and able to go on their journey.

The garden of the Wicked Prince's castle lay close to the Way of the King, but a high wall had been built by the

King's servants along the roadside, so that the savage dog could not see the pilgrims or come near to hurt them after they had passed through the Wicket-gate. A number of trees were planted in the garden, and their boughs hung over the wall and made a pleasant shade. Christiana did not know that the garden belonged to the castle, and she allowed the children to walk near the wall. Presently they saw that some of the trees were full of fruit, and as the branches were quite within reach, Matthew began to gather the ripe berries.

"You should not do that," said Christiana. "The fruit is not ours, and perhaps it is not wholesome."

"It is very sweet and nice!"

"I would not eat it if I were you."

James and Joseph were wise enough to listen to their sister, and they threw away the fruit that Matthew had gathered for them. But Matthew felt vexed and said to himself, "I am nearly as old as Christiana, and I know quite as much as she does. The fruit is very good!" So he went on eating it.

55

The First Trouble

The children were not far from the Wicket-gate when they saw two boys coming toward them. These boys were much taller than Matthew, their clothes were of bright-colored velvet, and they wore caps with little plumes fastened at the side.

"They must be princes," said little Joseph. "Has the King sent them to meet us?"

"I don't think the King's servants are ever dressed so gaily," replied Christiana. "And I am sure they cannot be princes from the Celestial City, for their faces are bad and ugly. Let us walk quickly and take no notice of them."

The boys were laughing and talking together, and when Christiana and the children came near to them they stood in the middle of the path and would not allow the little pilgrims to pass by. Matthew and his brothers were frightened, and Christiana scarcely knew what to do.

"We have no money to give you," she said. "We are quite poor children, and we are going to the King's city."

Then the tallest boy seized Christiana's hand, and his companion caught hold of Mercy. "Don't be frightened," they said. "We don't want your money, and we are not going to hurt you. You are two very pretty little girls, and you shall stay and talk to us for a while."

"We cannot," said Christiana. "We have no time to spare. Please let us go on."

"Oh, that is all nonsense!" replied the boys. "We shall not let you waste a lovely day like this in traveling. You need not pretend you will not stay with us, because we shall make you."

Perhaps if Matthew had not been eating the fruit from the Wicked Prince's garden he would have felt brave and would, at least, have *tried* to defend his sisters and Mercy. But I am sorry to say, he only stood trembling with fear, and when James and Joseph saw this they were frightened also and clung closely to him.

Christiana and Mercy saw that they would not be able to get safely away from these two boys, so they both cried out for help. And as they were not very far from the gate, Goodwill heard them and sent a man at once to see what had happened.

The man ran quickly and soon overtook the children. As he drew near he called to the boys, saying, "What are you doing? How is it that you dare to hinder the King's pilgrims?" When the boys heard the man's voice, they let Christiana and Mercy go free and hurried to the wall. They climbed it as fast as they could and dropped over into the Wicked Prince's garden. The children were very glad to see them disappear, and Christiana began to thank the man for his kindness in coming to help them.

"You need not thank me," he said, "but it is not well for little girls to travel alone. I was surprised that you did not ask Goodwill to send a guide with you. Your brothers are not old enough to be of much use."

Poor Matthew hung his head when he heard this and felt sadly ashamed of himself. He had intended to be so very brave, and he knew that he had acted like a coward.

"We never thought about the danger," said Christiana, "or that we should need a guide. I wish we had asked for one! Why did not Goodwill send someone with us if he knew that it was not safe for us to be alone?"

"The King does not allow him to send guides unless the pilgrims wish for them," replied the man.

"Perhaps we had better turn back again," said Christiana, "and tell Goodwill that we are sorry."

"No, you must not turn back. I will take a message to him, and then when you come to the house of the Interpreter you can ask for a guide there."

"Oh," cried Mercy, when the man had left them, "I thought we should never have any trouble again!"

"You did not know," said Christiana, "but I did, and I ought to have remembered that we are only girls and not able to take care of ourselves as well as little Christian was."

56

The House of the Interpreter

After this trouble, the children went on their way very steadily for some time. Matthew ate no more fruit, and James and Joseph held each other by the hand and kept nearer Christiana than they had done in the morning. Presently Innocence began to grow sleepy, and Mercy said that her feet were aching badly, so that all the little pilgrims felt very much pleased when they saw a large house in the distance standing close to the wayside.

"That must be the house of the Interpreter," said Christiana. "We must ask if we may sleep there, and do not let us forget to beg for a guide."

Now it happened that one of the King's servants, who had seen the children leaving the City of Destruction, had passed by the house of the Interpreter a little earlier in the day and had told his friends there of the new pilgrims who were on their way to the King's City. The Interpreter's children remembered little Christian, and they knew that he had been very sorry because Christiana would not come with him when he began his journey.

"This must be the same Christiana," said one of them. "How pleased little Christian will be when he meets her at the gates of the City!"

The windows were wide open, and as the little pilgrims came up the pathway to the door of the house, they could hear the children talking, and Christiana fancied that she caught the sound of her own name. She knocked timidly at the door, and a maidservant came to open it.

"Who is it that you wish to see?" she asked.

"We were told that this house belongs to one of the King's servants," replied Christiana, "and that he allows pilgrims to rest here. Do you think we may stay until the morning? For my little sister is tired, and we shall be afraid to go on traveling when it is dark."

Then the maid answered, "You must tell me your name, and I will ask my master whether there is room for you in the house."

"My name is Christiana. I knew little Christian, and I think he stayed here when he was a pilgrim. These are my three brothers, and this little girl is my friend."

The maid turned away and went quickly to the room where the children were sitting. "Can you guess who is at the door?" she cried. "Christiana herself, with her brothers, and her little sister, and her friend!"

The children were delighted and ran at once to find their father, that they might tell him the good news. The kind Interpreter was pleased also, and he hastened to the door and welcomed the little pilgrims with many gentle words.

"Are you really Christiana," he asked, "of whom little Christian told us when he stayed here?"

"Yes," she replied; "and I wish now that I had come with him, for I have found that all things he told me were quite true."

"You have done right to follow him," said the Interpreter. "But we must not let you stand at the door. Come in, my children, and you shall rest."

There were other pilgrims staying in the house, and two or three of the King's servants, as well as the Interpreter's own family. When the kind old man led Christiana into the large hall where they were sitting, everyone seemed pleased to see her. And although Innocence was a little shy at first, and Mercy was timid among so many strangers, they soon felt happy and at home.

57

The Man with the Straws

When the children had rested for a short time, the Interpreter took them to see his beautiful picture of the Good Shepherd. Even baby Innocence understood how the little lamb had been lost upon the mountains and had been in sad trouble until the Good Shepherd had found it and taken it in His arms.

After this the old man brought his little visitors into a dull, dark room, where a miserable-looking man was working busily. The floor of the room was covered with straws and sticks, and the man held a rake in his hand, with which he was collecting all the rubbish into a heap. He did not look up when the Interpreter opened the door, and he seemed to care for nothing but his sticks and straws.

"What is he collecting them for?" asked Matthew.

"He thinks they are very precious," replied the Interpreter. "He has been serving the Wicked Prince for a long time, and he believes that some day, in the midst of these useless straws, he will find a wonderful treasure. The King is sorry for him and every day He sends a messenger to offer him a golden crown instead of straws."

As the Interpreter spoke, he pointed upward. And when the children raised their heads, they saw above them, in the air, the beautiful figure of an angel, holding a bright crown in her hand.

"But he doesn't see it!" said Mercy.

"No," said the Interpreter, "he will not look up."

Tears came into Christiana's eyes. "I am afraid I was just like him," she said. "I did not care about the King and His City. But I *do* care now."

"Will he *never* look up?" asked James.

Joseph added, "How long will the angel wait for him?"

"I cannot tell you," replied the Interpreter. "The King is very merciful and very patient. But the man is so sure that he will find his treasure hidden in the rubbish that I do not know whether he will ever listen to the angel's voice."

They went next into the garden, where the beds and borders were all filled with flowers. The Interpreter told the children that the King's servants were like the flowers. Some plants are tall and stately, and no one can help seeing how beautiful they are. Others are quite tiny, and perhaps their blossoms are not even brightly colored, and have only a sweet scent. Still, the gardener loves *all* his flowers and puts each one in its proper place.

"In the same way," said the Interpreter, "the King loves all His servants and gives them each a place in His kingdom. Some have difficult and important work to do, and others have only simple work, but not one little flower is forgotten."

"Daisies are quite little flowers," said Mercy, "and so are violets, but they are very pretty."

"Yes," said the Interpreter, "and don't you think we love the violets as well as we love the roses? Children can be meek as daisies and sweet as violets, and the King will see them and love them."

It was now growing dark, for the sun had set, and presently the time came for supper. The Interpreter kept the children near to him and talked very kindly to them. He asked Christiana many questions about her old home and even persuaded shy little Mercy to tell him how she had seen the King's letter to Christiana and had made up her mind to be a pilgrim.

58

Greatheart

*I*n the morning the little pilgrims were awakened by the light of the rising sun. They all got up quickly and dressed themselves, for they felt very eager to continue their journey.

But when they came downstairs, the Interpreter called them to him and said, "These clothes that you are wearing will not do to travel in. We must give you some new ones out of the King's treasury."

' Christiana blushed. "I am so sorry," she said. "I washed and mended them as well as I could, but I know they are not nice."

"You did your best," replied the Interpreter kindly, "but even if they were quite new and clean, they would not be fit for you now. The King's pilgrims cannot wear garments that have been made in the cities of the Wicked Prince. Our good Prince has provided white robes for all His children, and the King will not receive you in any others."

When little Christian was traveling to the Celestial City, you remember how the Shining Ones met him at the Cross and clothed him in white. Christiana, and Mercy, and the boys, and even little Innocence, now received dresses that were just as spotless and beautiful as Christian's. And when they looked at each other the children were almost frightened. If the journey was long and difficult, how could they possibly keep such dresses clean until they reached the gates of the City?

James and Joseph stood quite still, gazing down at their snowy suits. "We can never play anymore!" they said.

The Interpreter smiled and drew the little boys nearer to him. "Do not be afraid," said he. "The King loves to see His children merry and happy. Your clothes will not be harmed, unless you quarrel or play in a naughty way. You may run about as much as you like, if you do not leave the Way of the King."

Christiana and Mercy were looking at each other with tears in their eyes.

"The King is very good!" said Christiana, but Mercy could not speak. All this time she had been afraid, because she had entered the Wicket-gate without receiving a message from the King. But now that she was clothed in garments from His own treasury, she felt that she was a true pilgrim, and she was ready to cry for joy.

When they were all prepared to leave the house, the Interpreter called one of his servants whose name was Greatheart and said to him, "You must go with these children to the Palace Beautiful and take care that none of the King's enemies come near to hurt or frighten them on the way."

Greatheart was a tall, pleasant-looking lad, not much older than Christiana. But he wore a suit of bright armor, and he carried a sword at his side, so that the children felt sure he would be able to protect them if they met with any danger. Innocence stretched out her tiny arms when she saw his brave, kind face. He took the little girl from Christiana, saying, "Let me carry her for a little way, and then she can run upon the grass until she is tired."

The Interpreter and his children came to the door and watched the little party set off: Greatheart carrying Innocence, while James and Joseph walked gravely hand-in-hand beside him; then came Christiana and Mercy, and, last of all, Matthew, whose head was aching, though he did not choose to say anything about it. The fruit that he had eaten the day before was poisonous and had done him no good. But the foolish boy was ashamed to own how ill he felt, so he walked on behind Christiana and hoped that the Palace Beautiful was not very far away.

59

A Rest by the Cross

*B*efore the day became hot, the pilgrims came to the Cross, and there Greatheart allowed them to rest. They all sat down upon the grass, and he told them how little Christian's burden had fallen from his shoulders at this very place. Then Christiana began to question him about the Prince and all that He had done for His servants. Greatheart loved the Prince and was very willing to talk about Him, so the minutes slipped quickly away, and the children felt almost sorry to leave their quiet resting place.

Not very far from the Cross they saw a sad sight. Do you remember how little Christian tried to awaken the three foolish boys who were lying on the grass by the wayside, with their feet bound in iron fetters? You know that they would not listen to him, and he was obliged to leave them. After a time they did wake up, but they never tried to undo their fetters, for they had no wish to continue their journey. All day long they sat idly by the road, doing everything they could to hinder the King's pilgrims by talking to them and trying to persuade them to forsake the right path. At last they did so much mischief that the King would have patience with them no longer, and He ordered them to be put to death. Their bodies were hung in chains, where pilgrims passing by could see them and take warning from their dreadful fate.

Greatheart did not allow little Innocence to look at the dead bodies, because she was too young to understand how naughty the three boys had been. But the other children saw them and asked what they had done.

Greatheart told them the whole sad story, and Christiana said, "I am glad they did not turn little Christian out of the Way."

"So am I," said Mercy, "and I think it was a very good thing that they were killed. If they had been left alive, and we had been obliged to make our pilgrimage alone, they might have hurt or frightened us very much."

The road now brought the children to the foot of the Hill Difficulty, and there Greatheart showed them the two paths that the Wicked Prince had made, one leading into the woods and the other into the dark mountains.

"Formalist and Hypocrisy were lost here," said he, "at the time when little Christian climbed the hill. Since then the

King has sent men to put posts and chains across the paths, so that His pilgrims may know they are not safe. But many pilgrims are so foolish that they take no notice of the chains, and try the paths because they look so easy, and then they are lost."

Just at the foot of the hill, and close to the Way of the King, there was a little spring of pure water. Greatheart pointed it out to the children, who were thirsty after walking in the sun. The water flowed into a tiny pool, and when Christian passed by this pool was as clear as crystal. But some of the Wicked Prince's servants, who were seeking for mischief to do, had found the spring, and they thought it would be a great thing to spoil it and make it unfit for the King's pilgrims to drink from. So they trampled down the edges of the pool until the earth fell into the water and made it too muddy for any one to drink. They did this whenever they passed that way, and when Greatheart brought his little band of pilgrims to the spring, he found it in a sad state.

But Christiana had packed a little cup in the bag that the boys were carrying, and Greatheart told them to fill the cup with water and let it stand for a few moments. Then the sand and soil sank to the bottom, and the water was left clear and bright. So they all drank of it and were much refreshed.

60

The Hill Difficulty

*T*he path up the hillside was very hard to climb. Greatheart carried Innocence, and the children helped each other as much as they could. But the way was steep and rough, and the sun's rays were beating fiercely upon them as they toiled along.

Presently Mercy exclaimed, "Oh, what a dreadful hill! I don't think I can walk another step. May we not sit down and rest a little?"

When Joseph heard Mercy's words he began to cry, for although he had been doing his very best to climb the hill like a brave boy, he had fallen many times, and his hands and knees were bruised and sore.

If Mercy is tired, he thought, *it cannot be very babyish of me to be tired too.* And then his weary little heart failed him, and the tears ran quickly down his cheeks.

"We will not stay here," said Greatheart. "We are very near to the arbor that the King has provided as a resting place for His pilgrims. Is that Joseph crying? Come to me, little one, and hold my hand. You have climbed bravely, and you must not cry now that we have passed over the worst part of the way."

Joseph felt happier when he heard Greatheart's words. He brushed away his tears and clasping his little fingers tightly around those of his kind guide, he stepped out briskly. In a few minutes the pleasant arbor came in sight, and the children hastened toward it.

"Oh!" cried Mercy, "it *is* good to rest when you are tired! Our King is very kind to make such a cool, shady arbor for His pilgrims."

"You see," said Greatheart, "our Prince has traveled over this path Himself, so He knows how hard it is, and how much the pilgrims need a resting place." Then, calling James and Joseph to him, he asked them how they liked their pilgrimage.

"I didn't like it at all just now," said Joseph, "but I am very much obliged to you for helping me."

"I think," said James, "that I would rather be going up-hill to the King's City than down again toward the Wicked Prince's country."

"Yes," said Greatheart, "and when you reach the King's City, you will be so happy that you will forget all the trouble you have had on your journey."

"Would you not like something to eat while you are resting?" said Christiana. "The Interpreter gave me some dried fruits and a piece of honeycomb."

She brought out the little store and divided it among them, asking Greatheart to take his share, but the lad refused, saying he would soon be at home again, where plenty of food would be prepared for him, but they were pilgrims and must make the most of what was provided for them.

61

The King's Arbor

The little pilgrims sat quietly in the King's arbor, eating their fruit and talking happily together, while Greatheart stood in the doorway, watching them.

"We must not rest too long," he said presently, "for we have still some distance to go, and the sun will soon be setting."

James and Joseph sprang up at once and started off hand in hand. All their bravery had come back again, and they whispered to each other that they would not mind *very* much even if they were alone.

"Greatheart says the King is so good, and we know He took care of little Christian," said Joseph.

"Yes," said James, "and if we love Him He will not let anyone hurt us. So I think we had better not feel frightened anymore."

When Christiana saw her two little brothers set off so quickly she made haste to follow them. The kind Interpreter had given her a bottle filled with refreshing drink, and she had not gone very far before she found that she had left this bottle in the King's arbor. James ran back to look for it, and while they were waiting for him Mercy said, "Did not Christian lose his Roll here? This seems to be a *forgetting* place!"

Greatheart smiled, and Christiana asked why pilgrims lost things in that arbor. "I remember," she said, "that I have heard of other pilgrims who have had to turn back here to look for something which they had left behind."

"It is only because they are careless," replied Greatheart. "They are tired with climbing the hill, and the rest in the arbor makes them feel comfortable and happy. Very often they are tempted to sit there longer than they ought to do, or they fall asleep, as little Christian did. They they start up in such a hurry that they are almost sure to lose something without noticing it."

James soon returned with the bottle in his hand, and the little pilgrims climbed steadily up the hill, until they reached the place where Mistrust and Timorous met Christian and frightened him by telling him of the lions. The two foolish boys were afterward caught and punished by the King's servants, and a stone was placed by the wayside, with some words written upon it advising pilgrims not to listen to persons who tried to persuade them that the Way of the King was too difficult or dangerous for them.

"But there are some lions, are there not?" asked Joseph.

"Yes," replied Greatheart, "but you need not be afraid of them."

Joseph looked at his brother, and the two little fellows clasped each other's hand more tightly.

"I don't know whether I *should* quite like to meet a lion," whispered James. "It might be a *very* savage one. We will try not to mind, but we had better keep close to Greatheart."

The sun had now set, and the shadows were deepening every moment. The lions were wide awake when the children came in sight, and they both stood up and roared very loudly. Poor little James and Joseph shook with fear, and they slipped behind Greatheart, who had drawn his sword and held it in his hand ready to strike the lions if they sprang forward. The great beasts were chained, but the path between them was very narrow, and the savage creatures sometimes tried to seize the pilgrims who wished to pass by them.

62

Giant Grim and the Lions

Greatheart soon missed the two little boys and looked round to see what had become of them.

"This is not right," said he. "You were running bravely on before us while there was no danger, and now you are hiding for fear of the lions! You must learn to trust in the King, and then you will not be so much afraid."

But all the children were frightened, and even Christiana felt glad Greatheart was with them. He looked so strong and brave.

"I don't know what we should have done," said Mercy, "if we had had no guide to go before us. Oh, do you see?" she added. "There is a terrible giant standing by the lions!"

The giant's name was Grim, and he had made a home for himself near to the Way of the King. He had taught the lions to obey him, and very often he came to feed them and to frighten any pilgrims who might be passing.

When he saw Greatheart he stepped into the narrow path and stood with his hands upon the necks of the two lions. Greatheart went boldly forward, but the children clung to each other and waited to see what would happen.

"What business have you to walk upon this path?" said the giant.

Greatheart answered, "I am taking these children home to the Celestial City."

"This is not the way to the City!" said Grim. "I shall not let you pass. My lions are very fierce, and I can make them tear you in pieces!"

As Christiana looked before her she saw that the path was all grown over with grass. The giant had frightened the

King's pilgrims so much that for many weeks scarcely anyone had dared to pass that way. They had forgotten that the King would take care of them. But Christiana remembered what Wisdom had told her before she left home, and she suddenly cried out, "We are only children, but we are not afraid! Our King will take care of us and will bring us safely past the lions!"

When the giant heard Christiana's voice and saw that it was only a girl who was speaking, he laughed and said that she should not go another step toward the King's City, for he and his lions could soon kill her and her companions.

Christiana clasped little Innocence very closely in her arms, and Mercy clung to her, scarcely daring to look up. The boys were all crying together—even Matthew, who had never felt brave or happy since he had eaten the fruit from the Wicked Prince's garden. But Greatheart kept on his way, and the children crept timidly after him.

His armor shone brightly before them in the midst of the shadows (for the daylight was nearly gone), and in a moment his sword flashed through the air, and the giant moved back a few paces.

"Do you think you can kill *me*?" he shouted.

"This path belongs to the King," said Greatheart. "Stand and defend yourself, for if you will not let these children pass, I will fight for them!"

63

Watchful Receives the Children

When Greatheart raised his sword to strike the second time, the giant stooped down to unfasten the chains of the lions. But before he could do this the sharp weapon crashed through his helmet, and he fell upon his knees. He tried to get up again, but the King helped His brave young soldier, and, after a short struggle, the terrible giant lay dead at Greatheart's feet.

Then the lad turned around to look for the little pilgrims. Mercy had hidden her face, but Christiana had watched the battle, though, when the giant shrieked with pain, she could not help trembling. Greatheart held out his hand to her.

"Come," said he, "there is no danger now. Keep close to me, and the lions will not hurt you. Their master is dead, and they are too much frightened to spring at anyone."

The children saw that the lions were cowering upon the ground, so they hurried past them and followed Greatheart to the gate of the Palace Beautiful. Watchful, the porter, looked out of his window and asked who was there.

"It is I!" said Greatheart. Watchful knew his voice, and, taking his lantern, he came quickly to the gate and opened it.

"How is it that you are so late?" said he.

"I have brought some little pilgrims from the House of the Interpreter," answered Greatheart. "We should have been here earlier, but the giant met us and wished to turn us back again. I had to fight with him, but the King helped us, and I have killed him."

"I am glad that he is dead," said Watchful, "for he has given us much trouble. You must come in and rest yourself."

"No," replied Greatheart, "it is late, and my master will expect me to return tonight."

"Oh!" exclaimed Christiana. "How can we ever reach the Celestial City unless you go with us?"

"Yes, indeed!" cried Mercy. "There are so many dangers, and we have no strength to fight with giants and wild beasts."

Matthew and Joseph were afraid to speak, but little James came close to Greatheart's side and clasped his hand, saying, "Do, please, go all the way with us!"

"I will go with you very gladly," said Greatheart, "but I must first ask leave of my master. You should have spoken to him this morning when we were setting out. I must go back tonight, but I will tell him what you say, and perhaps he will let me come to you again."

So he bade them all good night and was soon out of sight, for it was not quite dark.

Then Watchful turned to Christiana and asked her who she was and where she had been living. Christiana told him, and he was pleased to hear that she was Christian's friend. Everyone in the Palace liked the little boy, and they had not forgotten how lovingly he had spoken of Christiana.

Watchful rang his bell, and the maidservant who answered it went quickly back into the Palace with his message. Very soon Prudence and her sisters came out to welcome their new guests. Discretion had gone away to work for the King in another place, but her three daughters had the care of the Palace, and they received Christiana very kindly.

64

Mercy's Dream

"Supper is ready," said Prudence, as she led the children through the large hall, "so we will not tire you with talking tonight. You must sleep well, and tomorrow we shall like to hear all about your journey."

She looked so kind and she spoke so gently that Christiana took courage and said, "I don't know if I ought to ask for anything, but if you would let us sleep in the room where little Christian slept, we should be so very glad."

Prudence answered that no one was using the room, and she would be very pleased to let them have it. And there was also another little room opening into it, which she said she would give to the boys.

Christiana and Mercy lay awake for a long time, talking of all that had happened since they left the City of Destruction.

"I didn't think," said Christiana, "when little Christian used to tell me about the King, that I should ever be a pilgrim myself."

"No," said Mercy, "and you never thought you would come to stay in this grand palace and sleep in the very room that Christian slept in."

"I loved him so much!" continued Christiana. "He was just like one of my own brothers, and I felt so sorry when they told me that he had really gone away. But now I am happy again, for I know that he is with the King, and some day I shall meet him in the beautiful Celestial City!"

"Listen!" cried Mercy. "Is not that the sound of music? I am sure it is, and singing too. Did you ever hear anything so sweet?"

The children lay still, while below, in the hall of the Palace, the King's servants sang His praises before they went to rest. Little Innocence fell asleep in her sister's arms, and, when the music ceased, Christiana and Mercy whispered, "Good night," to each other and closed their eyes, feeling happier than they had ever felt before.

In the morning Christiana said, "Do you know you were laughing in your sleep? Did you have a dream?"

Mercy's eyes shone as she answered, "I had a lovely dream! Did I really laugh?"

"Yes, you wakened me. What did you dream about?"

"I thought I was sitting in a lonely place and crying because I felt miserable. A number of children came and teased me and wanted to know what I was crying for. Some of them laughed at me and pushed me, so that I cried more than ever. At last I looked up, and I saw a beautiful angel with soft white wings. He came straight to me and said, 'Mercy, what are you crying for?' I told him that I was very miserable. Then he spoke gently and wiped the tears from my face, and he gave me a dress all shining with silver and gold. He put a crown upon my head and took me by the hand, and we went on and on together until we came to a great golden gate. The angel knocked, and the gate was opened, and he took me in and brought me to a throne where the King was sitting. Oh, Christiana, He looked *so* kind and gracious! I didn't feel the least bit frightened, and He held out His hand to me, saying, 'Welcome, little daughter!' Everything was bright and twinkling, just like stars in the night, and I thought I saw little Christian, and then I woke. Are you sure I laughed?"

"Yes, and I don't wonder, when you had such a nice dream! I think it must be time for us to get up now, and we had better waken the boys!"

65

Pleasant Days

"Little Christian stayed here more than one night," said Mercy, while they were dressing. "If Prudence invites us, what shall you say? She looks so pleasant. I should like to make friends with her and with her sisters."

"We will see what they wish us to do," replied Christiana. "Perhaps all the pilgrims stay here for a few days."

After breakfast the three sisters began to talk to their new guests, and presently Prudence said, "We should like you to stay with us for a little while, if you think you can be happy here."

"Oh, yes!" answered Christiana. "We should enjoy it very much indeed."

The little pilgrims spent a whole month at the Palace Beautiful, and during that time many things happened of which I must tell you. Prudence and her sisters were very kind, and sometimes Prudence called the three boys together and questioned them to see what they knew. Christiana had tried to teach them about the King and His Son, and she was pleased to hear that they answered well.

"You must take pains to remember what your sister teaches you," said Prudence. "And when you hear older people talking of holy things, it will be right for you to listen, that you may learn more about the King and His goodness. And do not forget that the flowers and the birds and all the beautiful things around you were made by the King, and that there is a lesson for you to learn from even the humblest daisy or the tiniest fly. You are all so fond of reading," she continued, "and that is a good thing, but you may be sure that you will never find any better book that the King's own Book, the one which little Christian loved so dearly. There are stories in it for little children, and wise sayings for old people, and the more you read it, the more you will love it, for it will teach you how to serve the King faithfully."

Not far from the Palace lived a boy whose name was Brisk. He was a bright, good-natured lad, and Prudence hoped that he would one day be a true servant of the King. He often came to the Palace and talked to her, but she had never yet been able to persuade him to give up his careless ways and become a pilgrim. He always said he was too busy, but that some day he would find time to begin his journey.

When the little pilgrims had been at the Palace for about a week, Brisk came in one morning as usual. Mercy had a very sweet face, and when Brisk began to talk to her, he thought she was the nicest little girl he had ever seen. He asked her to come with him to see his brothers and sisters. But Mercy answered that she had a great deal of work to do, for she did not think that Prudence would be pleased if she left the Palace.

Brisk was so busy himself that he did not like Mercy any the less for being industrious, and he came to the Palace nearly every day that he might talk to her. Mercy asked her friends about him, and they told her that he had not yet learned to love the King, although he liked to come to the Palace and to talk with the pilgrims.

"He is a nice boy," said Mercy, "but he will not be a good friend for me if he does not love the King." So, whenever he came, she sat quietly sewing and did not take much notice of him.

66

Matthew's Illness

*B*risk was vexed when he found that Mercy did not care to talk to him, and one day he said to her, "You are *always* sewing!"

Mercy looked up smiling. "Yes," she said, "if I have no work for myself, there is always plenty to do for other people."

"You must earn a lot of money!" said Brisk.

"I don't do it for money," replied Mercy.

"What *do* you do it for, then?"

"I am making some clothes for Charity. She gives them away to people who are very poor."

"Oh!" said Brisk, and he looked so surprised that Mercy could not help smiling.

He did not come again to the Palace until the little pilgrims had gone, and when Prudence asked him why he had forsaken his friend, he replied that Mercy was very pretty, but she had such foolish ways.

However, Mercy was not sorry that he did not come. "I could not work so well when he was talking to me," she said, "and I don't wish for any friends who do not serve the King."

"That is right," said Prudence, stroking the child's soft hair. "You cannot help meeting boys and girls who are careless like Brisk, but it is wise not to have too much to do with them."

Christiana was now in great trouble. Matthew had been feeling ill all this time, and each day when he got up his head seemed to ache more, and he often felt so sick and faint that he could scarcely stand. At last he was obliged to tell his sister, and Christiana wondered what could have made him ill, for she had forgotten all about the fruit that he had eaten.

The next morning he could not lift his head from his pillow when Christiana came to waken him, and she made haste to finish dressing that she might ask Prudence what she must do. Prudence sent at once for a doctor, a grave old man named Skill. He was not long in coming, and Christiana took him up to see the sick boy. Matthew lay in bed, and Joseph sat near to him, for the brothers were very fond of each other.

"What has he been eating?" asked Skill.

"Nothing but wholesome food," said Christiana.

Skill shook his head. "He has been eating poison, and if the medicine I can give him will not take effect, he will die."

Poor Christiana was so troubled that she could not speak, but Joseph exclaimed, "Oh, don't you remember the fruit? It hung over the wall by the Wicket-gate, and Matthew would eat it, but you made us throw it away."

"Yes, he did," replied Christiana. "I told him not to take it, but I remember he would not listen to me."

"Ah!" said the doctor. "I was sure he had eaten something poisonous! And that fruit is worse than any other, for it grows in the Wicked Prince's own garden!"

The tears ran down Christiana cheeks, for Matthew lay upon the bed looking so white and still that she feared the doctor's words would come true, and that he would really die.

When Skill saw how frightened she was, he spoke to her gently. "Do not be too unhappy. I have one of the King's medicines with me, and if he has not eaten a great quantity of the fruit, it may do him good."

67

The Golden Anchor

*T*he medicine that Skill prepared was very bitter, and Matthew was too ill to care what anyone said to him. For a long time neither the doctor nor Christiana could persuade him to take it. But at last, after a great deal of trouble, he was made to drink it. Although for many hours he was in terrible pain, toward evening he began to grow easier, and Christiana was thankful to see him fall into a quiet sleep.

The next day he was able to get up for a while, but his illness had made him so weak that he could not walk without the help of a staff. Everyone was very kind to him, and Christiana's heart was full of thankfulness to the King for sparing his life.

"I should like to have some of that medicine always with me," she said. Skill was very willing to prepare some for her and told her how and when it should be used.

It was perhaps a good thing for Matthew that he had suffered so much, for he was now more ready to listen to his sister's advice. And, instead of thinking that he was too old to be taught by Prudence, he came to her as James and Joseph did and asked her about many things which he did not understand.

The time passed pleasantly away, and toward the end of the month Joseph reminded Christiana that she had wished Greatheart to guide them to the Celestial City.

"He was so good to us, and he is so brave," said the little boy. "How can we find out if the Interpreter will let him come?"

"I think I must write to him," said Christiana. So she wrote a letter that very day and gave it to Watchful, who sent a messenger with it to the House of the Interpreter. In the evening the messenger returned, saying that the Interpreter had read the letter and that he would send Greatheart to guide the little pilgrims on their journey.

Prudence and her sisters were sorry to part with the children, and in those last days they took care to show them all the treasures for which the Palace Beautiful was so famous. Among other things Christiana saw and admired a little golden anchor.

"You shall have it for yourself, if you like," said Piety. "You can wear it always, and, when you look at it, do not forget what it means."

"What does it mean?" asked Mercy.

"You know what is the use of an anchor. If it is firmly fixed the sailors do not mind how rough the sea may be. The anchor holds their vessel safely, though the waves may be tossing and the wind roaring all around them. So if you love the King, the hope that He will help you will keep your heart from failing. And, though you may be in the greatest danger or difficulty, you will never be really afraid."

The anchor hung upon a slender chain, and Christiana clasped it round her neck saying, "I shall be so glad to have it, for it will help us all to remember what you have taught us."

While they were talking, a knock was heard at the gate, and soon Watchful rang his bell and sent word that Greatheart had arrived. How pleased the children were to see him! Innocence ran at once into his arms, and, as he lifted her up, James and Joseph clung to him on either side.

"I have brought a gift for you from my master," said he, when the little ones had released him and he was able to speak to Christiana. He showed her a large store of dried fruit. "It can be easily carried, and you will find it useful when we are at a distance from any houses."

68

The Valley of Humiliation

*C*hristiana was much pleased at the Interpreter's kindness, and she had also to thank Prudence for making their stay at the Palace Beautiful so pleasant.

It was early when Greatheart arrived, and the children were not long in preparing for their journey.

"We will go to the bottom of the hill with you," said Prudence. "The path is slippery and rather dangerous."

As they passed through the gate, Christiana said goodbye to Watchful and asked him whether any other pilgrims had gone by that day. Watchful said no, but a man had rested in his lodge the night before and had told him of some pilgrims who had been attacked and robbed by the Wicked Prince's servants.

"But you need not be troubled," said he, "for our King's soldiers heard of it, and they pursued the robbers, and they are now in prison."

Christiana and Mercy had turned very pale when Watchful mentioned the robbers. But Matthew touched his sister's hand, whispering, "You need not be afraid, Christiana. You are forgetting that we have Greatheart with us."

So the little party set out and began to descend the steep path that led into the Valley of Humiliation. It was *very* slippery, but Piety carried Innocence, and Prudence gave a hand to each of the little boys, while Greatheart went first with Christiana, and Matthew came behind them all with Mercy.

At last they reached the valley in safety, and Piety said, "It was in this valley that Christian fought his battle with Self. But if that bad man comes out to meet you, you must not

be frightened. Greatheart will take good care of you, and the King will be ready to help you."

Then the sisters returned to the Palace, and the children followed their guide across the valley. It was a very lovely spot, and just at this time the ground was covered with lilies, which filled the air with their sweet scent.

"I should not have thought that the Wicked Prince or his servants would ever come here," said Christiana. "It is so very peaceful!"

"It is our Prince's favorite valley," replied Greatheart. "He once lived here for some time. But you must not expect to find any place where the Wicked Prince and his servants do not come until you are in the King's own country."

Presently Innocence began to clap her hands with delight, for at a little distance from the pathway she saw a number of sheep feeding, with the lambs frisking happily beside their mothers. A boy was taking care of them, but he was among the trees where he could not see the pilgrims, although they could see him. He was singing a merry little song.

"He is poor," said Greatheart, "yet he is happy. He works faithfully and knows that his master is pleased with him."

69

The Dark Valley

"Where did Self meet Christian?" asked James. "Shall we see the very place?"

"We shall come to it presently," replied Greatheart. "Self often meets pilgrims in that part of the valley. It is called Forgetful Green."

"Why?" asked Mercy.

"Because when pilgrims have been staying at the Palace Beautiful and are walking along this pleasant path, they often forget that the Way of the King is not *all* smooth and easy, and they begin to think that all dangers are past."

"Did Christian forget?"

"I think he did, but you know he loved the King very dearly, and he would not let Self persuade him to give up his journey."

It was not long before they reached the place where the battle was fought, and Greatheart told the story over again, for the boys loved to hear of little Christian's bravery and how wonderfully the King had helped him to overcome his enemy. Greatheart also showed them the rock by which the little wounded soldier had rested after the battle, and he told them of the beautiful dream that had comforted him so much.

The little pilgrims were now drawing near to the entrance of that Dark Valley. You remember Christian had to pass through that terrible place in the night. It was now early in the afternoon, and Greatheart hoped that he would be able to guide the children safely over the worst part before the darkness fell upon them.

It was always very gloomy in the Dark Valley, for the rocks were high and leaned toward each other, so that the sun could never shine upon the path below. Greatheart looked at the children as they drew closer to him. Mercy held Christiana's hand, and her lips were trembling. But Christiana pointed to the anchor that she wore upon her breast. And though their faces were pale, Greatheart knew that they were both thinking of the King and that they would follow Him bravely through the terrors of the valley.

James and Joseph were in great fear. The strange noises among the rocks and the dimness of the light frightened them more than the sight of the narrow, dangerous pathway. But Matthew made them walk before him and did his best to cheer and encourage them.

"Follow me carefully," said Greatheart, "and do not tremble, or you will miss your footing. Remember that the Shining Ones are near, though you cannot see them. And if you trust in the King, the Wicked Prince and his servants cannot harm you."

But poor little James had not gone very far before his feet suddenly slipped, and he would have fallen if Matthew had not caught him in his arms. Greatheart stepped back and, stooping down, lifted the child upon his knee. Christiana looked anxiously into his face, for she feared that someone had hurt him.

"He is only faint," said Greatheart. "If you will give him a little of Skill's medicine, he will soon revive."

The medicine was not nice, but Christiana persuaded the boy to take it, and presently he opened his eyes and began to feel better.

"I was frightened," he said. "I thought I saw horrible things. Will the King be angry?"

"No," replied Greatheart. "He knows how terrible this valley is and that you are only a little boy."

70

Terrors of the Way

*T*he Dark Valley was indeed a terrible place, and even Christiana grew timid and fancied that she could see strange shapes among the shadows. But Greatheart went steadily forward, and the little pilgrims followed him closely until they had passed half way through the valley.

Then Mercy, turning to look behind her, saw a lion coming after them. It began to roar as it drew near, and Greatheart made the children go before him, while he waited for the savage beast. But when the creature saw that its enemy was prepared to fight instead of running away, it crouched down upon the path and came no farther.

Soon after this, Greatheart himself was obliged to stop, for he found that the narrow path had been broken away, and a deep pit lay just before him. He did not know how to take the little pilgrims over it, for, although a tall active lad like Matthew might have been able to cross it, the girls and the little boys could not possibly have done so. And, all in a moment, while he was considering what to do, a thick mist rose up around them, so that they could not even see each other.

"This is dreadful!" cried Christiana. "What can we do?"

"We can only pray to the King," answered Greatheart. "He will not forsake us. Perhaps the pit is not a real one. The Wicked Prince has power in this valley to make us think that we can see dangers when they are not really there. We must stand quite still until the mist clears away."

The children obeyed, keeping hold of each other's hands, and praying in their hearts to the King to deliver them.

"It must have been worse for poor little Christian than it is for us," said Christiana presently. "He was alone, and he came through the valley in the night."

"The King was watching over him," said Greatheart. "I have brought many pilgrims along this pathway, and sometimes the danger has been far greater than it is now, but the King has always helped us, and we have been brought out safely."

Greatheart's words comforted the little pilgrims, and they waited patiently, although the strange noises and the sound of footsteps hurrying up and down were very terrifying in the darkness. But no one came near to hurt them, and after a time a light began to break through the mist. Soon it was clear enough to see the ground.

"It is as I thought," said Greatheart. "The pit was not real. See, the pathway is quite firm."

How thankful the children were, and how gladly they went on their way! But a new trouble soon came upon them. For some distance the valley was filled with a poisonous vapor, so that the air was scarcely fit to breathe.

"This is not a nice part of our pilgrimage." Mercy sighed. "I do not like it so well as staying at the Wicket-gate, or with the Interpreter, or at the Palace Beautiful."

"Ah," said Matthew, "but think how much worse it would be to live here always, as we might have to do if we served the Wicked Prince! Perhaps the King wishes us to pass through this dreadful place so that we may learn to care more about being with Him in the Celestial City."

"That is just the reason," said Greatheart.

"Shall we soon be able to see the end of the valley?" asked Joseph, for he was beginning to feel very tired and giddy with walking upon the narrow path.

"We are almost through," answered Greatheart, "but now you must be very careful, for we are coming to the snares."

71

The End of the Valley

I told you how little Christian was troubled by finding the ground near the end of the Dark Valley covered with snares placed cunningly up and down to entrap the pilgrims. Greatheart led his little company slowly along, but they found it very difficult to walk upon this dangerous path without falling or getting their feet entangled. Presently they saw the body of a man lying dead by the wayside.

"His name was Heedless," said Greatheart, "and he fancied he could walk safely here without the help of the King. But as he hurried carelessly along his feet were caught in a snare which threw him down, and his companion, who was called Take-heed, could not unfasten it."

"Did Take-heed escape?" asked Mercy.

"Yes, but it made him very sad to leave his friend in the power of the Wicked Prince."

You remember that just at the end of the valley Christian passed by the cave of the two old giants. They were both dead now, and a young giant had come to live in their cave. His name was Maul. He knew Greatheart and hated him very much and always tried to hinder him when he brought the King's pilgrims out of the valley.

As Greatheart drew near to the cave, Maul looked out, and seeing the pilgrims, he cried, "How often have you been forbidden to do this?"

"To do what?" asked Greatheart.

"You know what I mean," answered the giant angrily, "but I will put a stop to it." And, seizing his great club, he came down the rocky path toward the Way of the King.

"We will not fight," said Greatheart quietly, "until you tell me why you are attacking me."

"Because you are a robber," said the giant. "You carry off little children from the cities of my Prince and take them into a strange country, and no one knows what will become of them."

"I am a servant of the King," said Greatheart. "I am not a robber. My Master has commanded me to bring the children safely home to Him, and if you wish to fight me because I obey Him, I am quite ready."

When the giant heard this, he rushed suddenly upon the boy and struck him such a terrible blow with his club that Greatheart fell upon his knees. The poor little pilgrims gave a scream of fright, for they thought that their faithful guide would be killed. But Greatheart quickly sprang up again and wounded the giant's arm with his sword. After this they had a long struggle, while the children watched and trembled, for, although they knew that Greatheart was brave and trusted in the King to help him, they could see that the giant was young and very strong, and they feared he might gain the victory.

At last the giant became tired and would fight no longer, but he still refused to let Greatheart pass. He sat down by the wayside to rest, and Greatheart turned away and prayed to the King to give him new strength so that he might win the battle.

The little pilgrims prayed also. Maul saw what they were doing, and I think it made him feel afraid, for he knew that the King heard the prayers of His servants and that even little children had sometimes been able, by His help, to overcome the strongest giants. However, he determined to fight more fiercely than before, and he hoped that he would be able to kill Greatheart. If he could seize the little pilgrims and carry them back into the country of the Wicked Prince, he would receive a great reward.

72

Greatheart Overcomes the Giant

*T*he King did not forsake Greatheart. When the fight began again, the lad felt that his strength and courage were increasing every moment, and before long he succeeded in bringing the giant to the ground. Maul cried for mercy, and Greatheart allowed him to rise. But as he got up he struck at the young soldier with his club. The blow fell upon Greatheart's head, and if his helmet had been less strong it might have killed him. After that Maul's courage failed. Greatheart's sword had wounded him in his side, and he began to feel faint and could no longer hold his heavy club. It fell from his hands, and that ended the battle. In a few moments Greatheart was standing along upon the pathway, and the giant lay dead at his feet.

The children were full of joy, for, although the fight had been terrible to see, they knew that the giant was one of the King's enemies and that it was right for Greatheart to kill him. Near to the cave in which he had lived there were a number of large stones. The boys climbed up the rocks and rolled several of the stones down to the pathway. They built them up into a pillar, upon which they placed the head of the giant, so that pilgrims who came out of the Dark Valley might see it and know that their enemy was dead.

At a little distance from the cave there was a green mound overlooking the plain. From it Christian had seen Faithful, and when the children came to it, Greatheart advised them to sit down and rest and eat some of the fruit that he had brought from the House of the Interpreter. As they sat comfortably upon the grass, Christiana asked him whether he had been wounded.

"Not much," he replied. "My armor is so good. I have only a few cuts and bruises, which will soon be healed."

"Were you not frightened when the giant struck you with his club?" said Christiana.

"Yes, but I knew the King would help me. The Prince Himself has often been wounded, but He has always conquered in the end, and He will not let His servants be overthrown if they are faithful to Him."

It was now late in the evening, and although it was summertime, the light was beginning to fade, so the little pilgrims were obliged to hasten on their journey. Many fine oak trees grew upon the plain, and some of them stood quite close to the Way of the King.

As the children walked quickly along they saw a very old man sitting upon the ground under one of the trees. His staff was in his hand, but his eyes were closed, and he seemed to be asleep.

"He is dressed like a pilgrim," said Matthew.

"Yes, said Greatheart, "he is a pilgrim, but we must not leave him sleeping here."

He touched the man's shoulder to waken him, and the poor old pilgrim sprang up trembling, for he thought an enemy was trying to seize him.

"What is it?" he cried. "Who are you?"

73

Mr. Honest

Greatheart was sorry that he had startled the old man. "You need not be afraid of us," said he. "We are all friends."

But the pilgrim was not satisfied. He looked anxiously at Greatheart and Matthew and asked again who they were.

"My name is Greatheart," said the lad, "and I am taking these children to the Celestial City."

Then the man smiled, for he had heard of Greatheart before. "I was afraid that you were robbers," he said, "but I see now that you are the King's servants."

"What would you have done if we *had* been robbers?" asked Greatheart, for the stranger did not look fit to defend himself.

"I know I am only a feeble old man," he replied, "but I would have fought, yes, I would have fought as long as I had any breath, and I do not think even you two strong lads would have overcome me!"

"You speak like a good pilgrim," said Greatheart. "Will you not tell us your name?"

The old man shook his head. "Oh, never mind my name! I am only a poor fellow, and I used to live in a little place called Stupidity, about four leagues from the City of Destruction."

"Oh, is it *you*, Mr. Honest?" cried Greatheart, seizing his hand.

"Well, yes," he replied, "my name is Honest, but it is only by the help of the King that I can be true to it. How did you know anything about me?"

"I have heard my Prince speaking of you," said Greatheart, and then the old pilgrim's face flushed all over with pleasure, for he loved the Prince with his whole heart.

Like most good men, Mr. Honest was fond of children, and he soon made friends with the little pilgrims. They were pleased with his kind, good-natured face, and Christiana and Mercy thought that his long white hair was very beautiful. As for Innocence, she was quite ready to let him take her in his arms and kiss her.

As they went along in the twilight, Greatheart talked to Mr. Honest of his pilgrimage and presently asked him if he remembered one of his old friends named Fearing.

"Yes, indeed," said the old man. "I have often thought of him since the time when we lived near to each other. Has he reached the City safely?"

"My Master sent me with him from our house," replied Greatheart. "He was a very strange man, for, although he loved the King so dearly, he thought that he would be turned away from the gates of the Celestial City. He fancied that he was too weak and poor for the King to notice him and that he would not be helped as other pilgrims are. We were told that he stayed upon the plain for many days near the Slough of Despond, because he felt sure that he would sink in it. Many people offered to lead him over it, but he only wept, and though he watched them cross in safety, he would not venture."

"But he *did* cross," said Mercy.

"Oh, yes, after a long time! One bright morning he took courage, and when he reached the firm ground beyond the Slough, he could scarcely believe that the danger was really past. Then, at the Wicket-gate, he behaved in the same way. He did not think he would be received, so he would not knock. Other pilgrims came to the gate, and Goodwill let them in, but Fearing drew back, so that the porter never saw him. At last he crept up to the gate and gave one timid knock. Goodwill came at once, and, seeing no one, he stepped out upon the plain. Poor Fearing lay trembling on the ground, but Goodwill lifted him up and spoke kindly to him."

"I am sure he would!" said Mercy, for she remembered how she had been almost as timid herself before she entered the Way of the King.

"Goodwill is a kind friend to everyone," said old Mr. Honest. "But tell me how Fearing went on. I know very well what a strange man he was."

74

Fearing's Pilgrimage

*T*he rest of Fearing's story was soon told. Goodwill wrote a letter to the Interpreter, asking him to send a guide with the poor man from his house to the Celestial City. But Fearing spent several days and nights outside the Interpreter's gates before anyone knew that he was there. Then, one morning, Greatheart happened to see him from one of the windows and went down to speak to him. He was cold and weak for want of food, but he brought out his letter, and after a little trouble Greatheart persuaded him to enter the house.

"And you were with him always from that time?" said Honest.

"Yes. He was pleased when we came to the Cross, and he did not mind the Hill Difficulty or the lions. He was not afraid of such things. He only feared lest the King should not think him fit to be a pilgrim. At the Palace Beautiful he was very happy. He would not have much to do with the family or with their other guests, but he liked to hear them talk. You know there is a large screen in the hall, and he used to sit behind it, where he could not be seen, and listen to what was said. We stayed a long time in the Valley of Humiliation, for my Master told me not to hurry him, and he seemed to love the grass and flowers so much that he could not bear to leave them."

"How did he pass through the Dark Valley?"

"I was afraid it would be very terrible to him, and indeed it was. But the King did not allow him to be troubled as many pilgrims are. I never saw the valley so light or so quiet at any other time. In Vanity Fair he was very angry at the wickedness he saw around him. He was braver there than anywhere and was ready to fight the enemies of the King at every turn. However, we passed through the town without being hurt, and after traveling slowly for several weeks we came to the River."

"Was he not satisfied when he saw the gates of the Celestial City?"

"Not at first. He wandered along the shore, looking across at the bright walls and crying that he would never be received there. He was sure that he would be lost in the river. But when the message came for him, I went down to watch him crossing, and the water was so low that he went over quite easily. Then the Shining Ones met him, and I saw him no more."

Mr. Honest seemed very glad to hear of his old friend's pilgrimage and that he had reached the City safely. When Greatheart had finished his story, Christiana said, "I thought perhaps other pilgrims did not feel afraid lest the King should not receive them. I have felt in that way so often."

"So have I," said Mercy.

"I have too," said Matthew, "and I wondered whether the King would be displeased with me for it."

"No," replied Greatheart, "He will not be displeased. I think all good pilgrims feel anxious sometimes."

"If they were quite satisfied with themselves," said Honest, "it would show that they were not the King's true servants. I once traveled a little way with such a pilgrim. His name was Self-will, and he never troubled himself at all about pleasing the King. He thought he need only follow this path until he came to the City, and he would surely be received there."

While Mr. Honest was talking about this foolish pilgrim, a man passed by who said to Greatheart, "You must be careful, for there are some robbers out tonight upon this plain."

Greatheart was glad of the warning, and both he and Matthew kept watch as they went along. But they did not meet the robbers, who had perhaps heard of Greatheart and would not venture to attack him.

75

The House of Gaius

*I*nnocence was now sound asleep, with her head on her sister's shoulder, and the two little boys were beginning to feel fretful after their long day. The sun had set, and the stars were shining overhead, but Christiana did not like the thought of sleeping out of doors, and she asked Greatheart whether he knew of a house where they could rest.

"There is a friend of mine," said Honest, "a man named Gaius, who lives close to the Way of the King. We shall soon be in sight of his house, and I am sure he will give us a lodging."

Gaius received the little band of pilgrims very kindly. He always kept several rooms for the use of travelers, and his servants were as pleased as their master to have the chance of entertaining the King's pilgrims. While the cook was preparing supper, he brought his guests into his own parlor, where they were very glad to sit down and rest. He had much to say to his old friend Honest, and also to Greatheart, and the children listened quietly and felt very happy.

Presently a maid came in and spread a cloth upon the table and laid out the plates and bread. Then the cook sent up the supper, and the hungry travelers were thankful to see the good food placed before them—meat and potatoes, milk and butter and honey, and a dish of large rosy apples.

When Matthew saw the fruit, he blushed, for he thought of the poisoned apples that had made him so ill when he was at the Palace Beautiful.

"May we eat them?" he asked.

"Oh, yes!" replied Gaius, "they are wholesome fruit." Then Matthew told him why he was afraid.

"But those were poisoned apples," said Gaius. "These are from the King's orchards and will hurt no one."

After supper Gaius gave the boys some nuts to crack, and while they ate them he went on talking to Greatheart. At last Christiana thought it would be better for the little ones to go to bed, and she was also very tired herself. So Gaius showed her the rooms that had been made ready, one for her and Mercy and one for the boys, and before long they were all asleep in their comfortable beds. As for Mr. Honest, he was so pleased to see his old friend again that he would sit by the fire all night to talk to him, and Greatheart sat with him until the sun rose and the servants began to put the house in order for the day.

While they were at breakfast, Gaius told his guests of a wicked giant named Slay-good, who had come to live among the hills about a mile from his house.

"He is very strong and fierce," said Gaius, "but if you would go with me to attack him, I am sure the King would help us and give us strength to destroy him."

So Christiana and Mercy and the little ones were left to spend the morning quietly in the house, and Gaius took Greatheart and Matthew to look for the giant. Mr. Honest would go with them, for although he was very old, he was very brave, and he liked to see the King's enemies put to flight.

Now it happened that, the day before, the giant had seized a poor pilgrim named Feeble-mind, and, when Gaius and his party appeared, he was just preparing to kill him. But he was obliged to come out of his cave and defend himself when the little party of the King's servants began to attack him. Feeble-mind lay quite still in the darkness, and when he heard the sound of voices he rejoiced, for he felt sure that the King had sent someone to save his life.

The battle lasted for an hour, but Slay-good was overcome at last, and Gaius searched the cave carefully to see whether any captives were hidden there. Feeble-mind was soon found and carried back to the house, and when he had eaten some food, and rested a little, he was able to tell his story. .

76

Feeble-mind
and Ready-to-halt

*F*eeble-mind had never been a strong man, and he seemed scarcely fit to take a long journey.

"But," said he, "I have made up my mind that I will find the King's City, and if I am too weak to walk all the way, I will creep on my hands and knees! Everyone has been very good to me, and I have come thus far in safety. I could not have climbed the Hill Difficulty, but the Interpreter sent a servant with me, and he carried me on his back to the top of the rocky path. This is the worst thing that has happened to me, but as I lay in the giant's cave last night, I prayed to the King, and I felt sure He would save me. And you see He *has* saved me!"

Gaius had a daughter whose name was Phoebe. She wished very much to go to the Celestial City, and her father thought that it would be pleasant for her to travel with Christiana and Mercy. So they stayed a few days, while she prepared for her journey. On the last day Gaius made a feast for them, and when it was over Greatheart asked what he must pay for their lodging. But Gaius would not take any money. He said he loved the King and for His sake he kept his house open to any pilgrims who chose to stay there.

When the children were saying good-bye, Greatheart saw Feeble-mind standing silently in the doorway, and he said to him, "Are you not coming with us? The King will be glad for us to help you on your way."

Feeble-mind shook his head. "I am afraid I should hinder you," he replied. "You are all strong and active, and I am so weak! Then I am not merry as these children are, and I should make them feel sad with my dull ways."

"Oh, no, you will not!" cried Christiana. "Do come with us, and we will cheer and help you."

"Yes," said Greatheart, "it is not wise for you to travel alone. We shall be grieved if we have to leave you behind."

The tears came into the poor man's eyes, but he could not make up his mind to go with Greatheart, for he was really afraid of hindering the little pilgrims by his weakness. However, while they were all standing together on the pathway, they heard the sound of footsteps approaching, and another pilgrim came in sight. His name was Ready-to-halt. He was quite a lad, but he was so lame that he had to walk with crutches. When Feeble-mind saw him, he exclaimed, "Oh! how did you come here?" for he had known him before.

The lad smiled as he held out his hand. "How did *you* come up here?" he said. "I think we are both bound for the same place."

"You are lame, and I am weak," replied Feeble-mind, "but the King will not turn us away from the gates of His City. I was just wishing for a companion, and no one could suit me better than you."

"I shall be only too glad to go with you," said Ready-to-halt.

Then Greatheart and Mr. Honest spoke to him, and soon everything was settled pleasantly.

"We cannot travel very fast," said Greatheart, "and if you are not able to keep up with us, we can always wait for you."

So the little party set off once more. Mr. Honest walked first with Greatheart, and Matthew and his two brothers followed him. Then came Christiana and Mercy and Phoebe with little Innocence, and last of all the lame boy and Feeble-mind.

"I am sure we shall be able to help each other," said Ready-to-halt, "and when you are tired I will lend you one of my crutches."

77

Crossing the Plain

*T*he pilgrims spent the day in crossing the plain, and after walking for several hours they saw the walls and gates of Vanity Fair in the distance before them. The great towers rose darkly against the clear sky, and Christiana began to feel timid as she drew near the city of the Wicked Prince.

"It is such a dreadful place!" she said.

"Did not poor Faithful die there?" asked Mercy.

"Yes," answered Phoebe. "The people treated him very cruelly, and they kept little Christian in prison for some time."

"Do you think that *we* shall be put in prison?" said Mercy.

Christiana's face grew white, and she clasped Innocence more closely in her arms. "If we are separated from each other," she said, "do not let us forget all that has happened while we have been together. The King has been very good to us, and we know that He is always watching over us. If we have to suffer, we must be brave and patient because we love Him."

Feeble-mind and Ready-to-halt were walking just behind the girls and could hear all they said.

"Are you afraid?" asked Feeble-mind.

"I think we are," replied Christiana.

"Shall we be obliged to pass through the city?" said Mercy. "Is there no other way?"

Ready-to-halt looked kindly at the trembling little girl. "We might go round," he said, "but then we might not find our way into the right path again."

"I think we must go straight on," said Phoebe. "I have heard my father say that the people are less rough than they used to be. The Prince has told them to make things seem pleasant in the city, so that the pilgrims may feel inclined to give up their journey."

Greatheart and Mr. Honest turned around at this moment and waited for the rest of the little party to overtake them.

"We shall have to spend the night in Vanity Fair," said Greatheart, "for if we pass straight through the city, we shall not be able to reach another safe resting place before the darkness comes on."

"Where can we sleep?" asked Christiana. "Will not the people ill-treat us?"

"I think not," replied Greatheart. "I have brought many pilgrims safely through the city, and I know an old man who will give us a lodging and be very pleased to see us."

"Does he love the King?" asked Mercy.

"Yes. The King has commanded him to live here, so that he may keep an inn for the use of pilgrims."

"Why did not Christian and Faithful go there?"

"The city was more dangerous then, and it was not safe for any of the King's servants to live in it. But now that the people have grown quieter, they have allowed a few good men to build houses in the Fair."

"What can they do in such a place?" said Matthew. "Is it not wrong of them to live there?"

"No. The King has given them work to do for Him even in this wicked city. They help and protect the pilgrims who are passing through it, and when any of them are tempted to stay here, these servants of the King search for them and try to persuade them to continue their pilgrimage."

"Oh," said Christiana, "it is comforting to hear of this! We were feeling so frightened, for we thought that the people might put us in prison or even kill us, as they killed Faithful."

"They will not kill you," said Greatheart, "and if we pass quietly through the streets they will not try to hinder us."

78

In Vanity Fair

*I*t was a bright summer evening, and the city looked very beautiful in the light of the setting sun. The buildings were all large and grand, gay flags fluttered upon the towers and housetops, the people wore rich clothes, and even little boys, no older than James and Joseph, were dressed in suits of silk and velvet and wore large caps with long drooping feathers.

"I should like one of those caps!" whispered Joseph.

Phoebe heard the whisper, and she took the child's hand in her own. "Don't be foolish, Joseph," she said. "The gay clothes do not make the boys any happier. Your white dress is really more beautiful than the brightest of these, and you know you could not be received at the gates of the Celestial City if you wore clothes belonging to the Wicked Prince."

The town was less busy in the early part of the evening than at any other time of the day. The boys and girls were most of them tired of playing and lay idly in sunny corners, talking and teasing each other. They laughed at the pilgrims, but they did not crowd around them or try to prevent their passing through the streets, and even the men and women took very little notice of them. They soon reached the marketplace, where poor little Faithful had suffered. After crossing this wide space, Greatheart led them into a quiet street and stopped before the house of his friend whose name was Mnason.

Mnason had no sons of his own, and he was always pleased to see Greatheart. "Come in! Come in!" he cried. "You know that you are welcome! How far have you traveled today?"

"From the house of Gaius," replied Greatheart, "and it has been so hot upon the plain that we are all tired and shall be very glad if you can give us lodging and some food."

"I will give you the best I have," said Mnason. He led them into a large, cool room, where they could sit quietly and rest while he ordered a meal to be prepared for them.

When the supper was nearly ready, the kind innkeeper called his eldest daughter, Grace, and desired her to go to the houses of the King's servants and tell them that some pilgrims had arrived in the Fair and were staying with him. Grace did so, and presently several of these good people came in, and the evening was spent in talking of the King and of all that He had done for Christiana and her companions.

In the morning Mnason begged Greatheart to remain at his house for a few days, and when these were past a message was brought from the King desiring the pilgrims to stay in the city for some weeks longer.

Mnason and his two daughters, Grace and Martha, were very kind to their guests, and the children soon found friends among the King's servants. As for old Mr. Honest and Feeble-mind and the lame boy, they were all glad to have a long rest before continuing their journey.

The boys were able to make themselves useful in many ways, and the girls spent their spare time as they had done at the Palace Beautiful in sewing for the poor.

For, although most of the people in Vanity Fair were richly dressed, there were some who had wasted all their money and were clothed only in rags, and these miserable creatures were very thankful to anyone who could help them. Grace and Martha used to visit many of them and take them food and new garments and tell them of the King and His goodness. Christiana and Mercy and Phoebe were glad to help in this good work, so that the days they spent in Vanity Fair were both busy and happy.

79

The Great Dragon

Near to the city of Vanity Fair there was a large forest, and in this forest lived a terrible dragon. It was a fierce and cruel creature, and the people were very much afraid of it. It was so bold that it often came into the midst of the town and attacked both men and women, and sometimes it seized little children and carried them away to its den.

The servants of the Wicked Prince hated this dragon, but none of them were brave enough to resist it. When they heard its roaring, they fled away and tried to hide themselves, so that the savage creature grew more and more bold in its attacks upon them. But the servants of the King had made up their minds to destroy it if they could, and when they heard that Greatheart was staying at the house of Mnason, they determined to ask him to go out with them.

Greatheart was very willing to help them, and one morning the little party went forth in search of the dragon. It came out of the forest to meet them and did not seem to be in the

least afraid of them. Indeed it was so strong that it could easily have killed them all if they had not been armed with the King's weapons. However, they fought against it with all their might, and although they were not able to hurt it much in the first battle, they drove it back into its den, where it lay for several days, angry and frightened, and did not venture to approach the city.

While Greatheart stayed in Vanity Fair, he went out three or four times with the King's servants to fight the dragon, and before he left the city they succeeded in wounding it so that much of its strength and power were lost. You may be sure that the townspeople were very glad when they knew this, and that even the wicked men could not help honoring Greatheart and his companions for their bravery.

At last the time came for the pilgrims to continue their journey. Their friends were very sorry to part from them and gave them many presents.

Grace and Martha, Mnason's two daughters, had been waiting for a guide to take them to the Celestial City, so their father asked Greatheart whether he would allow them to travel with Christiana. Greatheart answered that it would be very pleasant for them to do so.

Many of the King's servants came to the gates of the city to bid the pilgrims farewell, and Christiana could not help thinking how good the King had been in making everyone so kind to her and her companions.

"We might have been treated no better than Christian and Faithful were," she said to Mercy. "I was really very much afraid that we should be put in prison, but you see we have found friends even here, and the King has kept us safely in the midst of this wicked city."

80

Christiana Leaves Innocence at the House in the Valley

The beautiful Valley of Peace was only a day's journey from Vanity Fair, and the pilgrims spent the next night in its quiet meadows.

In the morning Greatheart told Christiana that the King had built a house in this valley where the baby-pilgrims were nursed and taught by kind and good women until they were old enough to travel to the Celestial City.

"Do you mean that I ought to leave Innocence there?" asked Christiana.

"It will be wise for you to do so," answered Greatheart. "She is too young to spend all her days in traveling, and you know how hard the path is for her tender little feet."

"But I can carry her," said Christiana.

"Not all the way," said Greatheart, very gently, for he saw the tears in the girl's eyes. "I am sure you love Innocence, don't you?"

"Yes."

"The King loves her even more than you do, and He thinks it is better for His little ones to gain strength and wisdom in this quiet valley before they set out on their journey."

"Shall I have to go into the City without her? I thought we should all pass through the gates together."

"No. The King generally sends for His pilgrims one by one. Innocence will very likely come to live with you in the Land of Delight. But even if you have to cross the River without her, you need not be troubled, for you may be quite sure that she is safe and happy. I will take you today to see the King's house."

227

Poor Christiana felt very sad, but she loved the King too well to disobey Him. And when she had seen the kind women who nursed the little pilgrims, and the sunny rooms and beautiful gardens in which they lived, she grew more content.

The next day she carried Innocence across the meadows and led her up the pathway to the door of the King's house. A gentle-looking nurse came out to meet her, and Christiana said, "I have brought my little sister, for Greatheart thinks she is too young to travel any farther with us."

The nurse saw the tears in Christiana's eyes, and she answered, "You do not like to part with her!"

"No. I have no other sister, and I thought we could always be together."

"Dear little girl!" said the nurse. "I do not wonder that you love her. She will be very happy here, and it will not be long before she is strong enough to follow you."

Then she took Innocence in her arms and asked Christiana to come into the house with her. Christiana stayed there all day, and in the evening when she had seen Innocence sleeping peacefully in her little cot, she went back again through the valley to the place where the other children were staying.

Greatheart came part of the way to meet her, and he was so kind and gentle that Christiana felt comforted.

"I know the King's servants will teach her better than I can," she said, "and the path is very rough sometimes."

"Yes," replied Greatheart, "and you cannot carry her always. It is right that she should learn to walk alone. When you see her again, you will feel very glad that you trusted her to the care of the King."

Then he told Christiana that the King's Son, the good Prince whom they all loved so dearly, came very often to see the children and spent much of His time in teaching them and in leading them up and down in the broad meadows.

"When they are tired He carries them tenderly in His arms."

81

Doubting Castle

When the little pilgrims reached the stile that led into By-path Meadow, they saw the stone that Christian and Hopeful had placed by the wayside. The children were tired with walking, for that part of the road was very rough, so they sat down to rest for a little while and soon began to talk about the dreadful giant Despair.

"Why does not someone kill him?" asked Joseph.

"*We* are not strong enough, are we?" said James, looking at Greatheart. "But *you* could kill the biggest giant, couldn't you?"

Greatheart smiled. "Only with the help of the King," he answered, "and the King would help you if you trusted in Him."

"So that we could kill even Giant Despair?"

"Yes."

"Let us try!" exclaimed Joseph, eagerly. "He was very cruel to little Christian."

"Perhaps there are some pilgrims shut up the castle now," said Mercy.

"But is it not wrong to leave the Way of the King?" asked Christiana.

"If the boys really wish to fight with Giant Despair, the King will not be displeased," answered Greatheart. "Christian and Hopeful went into the meadow for their own pleasure, and so they fell into trouble."

"Then do you think we *may* go?" asked Matthew.

"Yes, if you are ready to fight like brave soldiers."

The boys were only too eager to follow Greatheart to Doubting Castle, and old Mr. Honest said that he must certainly go with them. Feeble-mind and Ready-to-halt would not have been able to fight, so they stayed by the wayside with Christiana and the other girls.

The little party was soon out of sight, and it was quite late in the day when it returned. They were full of triumph, and they brought two poor pilgrims with them, whom they had rescued from the cruel giant. One was an old man with a sad and weary face. He had been lying for many weeks in a dark dungeon, and even the gray evening light seemed to dazzle his weak eyes. He looked pale and faint, and when he had been brought safely into the Way of the King, he had to lie down upon the grass while Christiana and her friends rubbed his cold hands and fed him with wholesome bread and wine.

Presently he revived a little and was able to sit up and thank his deliverers. He told them that his name was Despondency and that he had been traveling to the Celestial City with his daughter, Much-afraid. The poor girl had done her best to comfort her father in his distress, but they had both lost all hope of being saved and could scarcely believe that Greatheart was a servant of the King and that they were really free once more.

"Did you kill the giant?" whispered Mercy to Matthew.

"Yes, and his wife too. She was very cruel, and she deserved to die as well as her husband. Oh, Mercy, the castle was such a dreadful place!"

"I am glad *we* did not fall into the giant's hands," said Mercy. "That poor girl looks as if she would die even now."

"She will soon grow stronger if we take care of her."

"Did you destroy the castle?"

"We broke down all the gates and doors."

"You must have been frightened at the giant."

"He was very rough and savage, but we prayed to the King, and even little Joseph fought bravely. It was our first real battle!" and the lad's eyes shone as he put his sword back into its sheath.

82

The Delectable Mountains

Greatheart had now quite a large party of pilgrims under his care. Good Mr. Honest took charge of Mr. Despondency, and Much-afraid, although she was older than any of the other girls, was very glad of their pleasant company.

The Shepherds, who lived upon the Delectable Mountains, saw the pilgrims coming toward their tents and were very pleased to find that Greatheart was with them. All the King's servants knew and loved him for he was such a gentle and faithful guide.

It was a clear, bright night, but as Despondency and his daughter were so weak after their long imprisonment, Greatheart thought it wise to remain with the Shepherds until the next day.

These kind men welcomed the whole party to their tents, gave them food, and prepared beds for them, so that in the morning they rose up refreshed and strengthened.

The Shepherds were always very glad when any of the King's pilgrims came to stay with them, and they liked to take their visitors to see the view of the Celestial City and the many strange places upon the mountains.

Christiana and her friends enjoyed their walk upon the hills very much, and when they had seen all the wonderful sights that had been shown to Christian and Hopeful, there was still a little time to spare before they continued their journey. So instead of turning back to the tents, the Shepherds led the pilgrims to a very beautiful hill called Mount Innocence.

Not far from where they stood, a man was walking upon the green slope. He was clothed in white, and his garments had not a single spot or stain upon them. But while the pilgrims watched him, two other men came across the mountain, and when they saw the man's white robes, they filled their hands with earth and began to pelt him with it.

"Oh," cried the children, "they will spoil his beautiful clothes!"

"No," said the shepherds, "the King will prevent that."

And, as the man came nearer, the pilgrims saw that the dirt, although it struck his clothes, fell from them without leaving the slightest stain.

"There is a lesson in that!" said Mr. Honest.

"Yes," said Greatheart, "a very good lesson for all pilgrims. When wicked people speak evil of them, they need not be unhappy, for the King will not allow false words to do them any real harm."

"And you may remember also," said the Shepherds, "that it is only by your own fault that the clothes which the King gives you can be stained. None of your enemies have any power to spoil them."

After this the Shepherds took their visitors to Mount Charity. A good man lived there whose work was to provide garments for some of the King's servants who were very poor indeed. He showed the pilgrims a wonderful roll of cloth that the King had given him to use. Every day he cut from it as many garments as were needed, and yet the cloth never came to an end.

"It is very strange!" said Christiana, as she watched the man at his work.

"The King's power and goodness are so wonderful!" said the Shepherds. "Those who really try to help His poor servants may be sure that their stores will never fail."

83

The Wonderful Glass

*A*lthough the Shepherds lived in tents during the summer, they had also a large and beautiful house, which the King had given into their care in order that it might be used as a place of rest for His pilgrims. When the children returned from their walk upon the mountains, they found dinner prepared for them in this house, and as soon as the meal was over, Greatheart desired them to get ready for their journey.

Mercy had eaten very little dinner, and she looked so pale and sad that Christiana whispered, "What is the matter, Mercy? Are you ill?"

Tears came into Mercy's eyes, but she shook her head and said nothing.

"What is it? asked Christiana. "Don't cry! Tell me what is troubling you."

"It isn't right for me to wish for things," said Mercy, with a little sob, "but you have your beautiful anchor, and I saw something just now that I should *so* like to have!"

"What did you see? Perhaps it is something that we may ask for."

"It is a glass in the dining room. I looked at it before dinner. You can see yourself in it, but when you turn it round, you don't see yourself anymore, but our dear Prince instead. It is so beautiful! There is the crown of thorns upon His head, and He seemed to smile at me, and I feel as if I could not be happy unless I had it."

Christiana felt puzzled. "The Shepherds are very kind," she said. "Perhaps if they knew you wished for it, they might be willing to let us have it."

"I could buy it, you know," said Mercy. "I have a little money."

"Well, don't cry anymore. I will ask the Shepherds about it."

So Mercy dried her tears, and in a few moments Experience came toward her. He spoke very gently and laid his hand kindly on her shoulder. "Christiana says that you have seen something in our house that you would like to have for your own. Tell me what it is, and the King will be very glad that we should give it to you."

Shy little Mercy blushed very much, but she looked up at the Shepherd and answered, "It is the glass in the dining room, in which you can see the Prince."

Sincere had followed Experience, and when he heard what Mercy said, he went at once into the house and brought out the glass. Mercy scarcely knew what to say when it was placed in her hands, but the Shepherds saw how timid she was, and they understood quite well that she was too happy and grateful for many words.

Then these kind men brought out of their treasures a present for each of the pilgrims, and, after wishing them a pleasant journey, they watched the little party until all were out of sight.

You remember that Christian and Hopeful received a map of the country and that the Shepherds gave them directions. Christiana and her companions did not need any map, because Greatheart was with them, and he knew the Way of the King and could warn the pilgrims when they came to any dangerous places.

84

Mr. Valiant

When Christian and Hopeful were traveling together, Christian told his friend the story of Little-faith, who had foolishly lain down to sleep by the wayside and had been robbed by some wicked boys. Greatheart and the pilgrims came presently to the very place where Little-faith had slept. It was at the corner of a lane, which led out of the Way of the King into the country of the Wicked Prince.

As they drew near, they saw a man standing alone, with his sword in his hand and his armor stained with blood. Greatheart stopped and asked him what had happened. The man was tall and strong, with a brave, handsome face, and as Christiana looked at him, she felt sure that she had seen him before.

"My name is Valiant," he answered, "and I am a pilgrim. Three men came down this lane and attacked me as I was passing. They said I might take my choice of three things, either to join them in robbing the King's pilgrims, or to go back to my own city, or to be put to death on this spot."

"What did you say to them?" asked Greatheart.

"I told them that I had always tried to be honest, and I certainly should not become a thief now. And that, as for my own city, I should not have left it if I had been happy there, but it was a bad place, and I had forsaken it forever. Then they asked me if I wished to lose my life, and I said my life was worth too much for me to give up lightly and that they had no right to meddle with the King's servants in such a manner. So they drew their swords, and I drew mine, and we have been fighting for nearly three hours. They have wounded me, but I think I wounded them also. And I suppose they must have heard your steps in the distance, although I did not, for they suddenly turned and fled away, and then I saw you coming."

"That was a hard battle, three men to one," said Greatheart.

"Yes," replied Valiant, "but I knew I was fighting against my King's enemies, and that gave me courage."

"Did you not cry for help? Some of the King's servants might have been near enough to hear you."

"I cried to the King Himself, and I am sure He answered me. I could not have fought so long in my own strength."

Greatheart smiled. "You are one of our King's true servants! Let me see your sword. Ah, yes, this is from the right armory!"

"It is a good sword," said Valiant. "No man who has so fine a weapon need be afraid, if he has learned how to use it skillfully."

"And you fought for three hours?" said Greatheart. "Were you not ready to faint with fatigue?"

"No, I fought until my sword clung to my hand, as if it were a part of my arm. But I think that made me feel stronger."

"You have been very brave!" answered Greatheart. "You must finish your journey with us. We shall all be glad of your company."

Mr. Honest, and Mr. Despondency, and the children all joined in welcoming the brave soldier. Christiana washed his wounds, and Mercy and Phoebe helped her to bind them up. After this they brought him food and wine and made him rest for a little while. Then, as the evening was coming on, they started once more on their journey.

85

Little Christian's Father

*C*hristiana was walking just behind Greatheart and Mr. Valiant, and she could hear all that the soldier said in answer to the questions of the young guide. She was still wondering where she had seen him before, when she heard him say that he had once lived in the City of Destruction.

"What made you become a pilgrim?" asked Greatheart.

"I had a little son," replied Valiant, "and when he knew that his mother was living with the King, he never rested until he had found out how to follow her. He went away one morning, and we did not miss him until it was too late for us to overtake him and bring him back."

"What was his name?" asked Greatheart. And Christiana listened eagerly for the answer, for she felt sure now that she knew who the soldier was.

"Christian," he answered. "I was very grieved when I heard what had happened, and it was many months before we had any certain news of him. Then a man named Truth came to the city, and he met me one day and told me how my brave little boy had traveled safely along the Way of the King and had reached the Dark River, and crossed it, and had been received by the Shining Ones at the gates of the Celestial City. He told me also that the child and his mother were living happily in the presence of the King, and when I heard this I began to feel restless and sad. The service of the Wicked Prince was no longer pleasant to me, and I forsook him and became a pilgrim."

"Did you come in at the Wicket-gate?"

"Yes, for Truth had told me that I could not be received by the King unless I did so."

Greatheart turned round and looked at Christiana with a smile.

"You see," he said, "the King has fulfilled little Christian's wish."

Then Valiant turned also. "Did you know my little boy?" he asked.

Christiana answered with tears in her eyes, for she knew how the child had longed for his father to follow him.

"Ah!" said Valiant, "it will give him great pleasure when he comes to the gates of the City and finds so many of his friends are waiting to enter!"

Greatheart and the soldier went on talking for some time, and Christiana listened to Valiant's account of his pilgrimage. He had always been very brave and diligent in his work, so that his master, the Wicked Prince, had been very unwilling to lose so good a servant. His companions had done everything they could to keep him at his post in the City of Destruction, and they had tried to frighten him by telling him of the dangers he would meet if he became a pilgrim. They told him of the fierce giants, and the lions, and the Hill Difficulty, of the Enchanted Ground, and the net of the Flatterer, and of the Dark River, over which there was no bridge and which must be passed before he could enter the Celestial City. They reminded him also of the many pilgrims who had gladly returned to their homes after venturing a long distance upon the Way of the King. And they declared that the story of his little son's happiness was not a true one, for they knew that he had certainly been lost in the Dark River and had never reached the opposite shore at all.

"Did not all these things discourage you?" asked Greatheart.

"No," replied Valiant, "I felt that Truth could not possibly be deceiving me, so I left the city and began my journey."

"And you have not been sorry?"

"No, indeed! I have met with many enemies, but I have trusted in the King, and He has helped me to conquer them all."

86

The Enchanted Ground

*A*lthough the Enchanted Ground was a pleasant place in which pilgrims were tempted to rest after the toils of their journey, they sometimes found the path across it full of difficulty and trouble.

The air was so warm and still that it made everyone feel sleepy, and the servants of the Wicked Prince had built many little arbors in the hope that foolish pilgrims would lie down to rest in them and so fall into the hands of their enemies. They had also planned a number of briars close to the Way of the King, and these had flourished so well that their long prickly branches were trailing all over the pathway, and Christiana and her companions had to pick their way among them very carefully indeed.

There had been a heavy storm of rain in the early morning, which had left the path soft and wet. Between the mud and the thorns the poor children began to feel quite faint and discouraged.

Greatheart and Mr. Valiant did their best to cheer the weary little company. Greatheart went first and made Feeblemind lean upon his arm. And Mr. Valiant came last of all, leading Mr. Despondency, who was still weak and unable to get on comfortably by himself.

Soon they passed by a large and very beautiful arbor, and I think if the children had been alone they might have been tempted to enter it. The walls were neatly made, and the roof had been covered that morning with fresh green boughs, which made it look cool and pleasant. But the pilgrims had learned to trust their wise young guide, and he had warned them that they must not think of sleeping until they had safely crossed this dangerous plain.

Night came on while they were in the midst of the Enchanted Ground, and this made traveling more difficult, for the air was damp and foggy, and the moon was not shining. However, Greatheart led them slowly along, and presently he desired them to stand still for a few minutes.

"We are coming to a place where several paths lead out of the Way of the King," said he, "and it is so dark I must look carefully at my map, or we may turn out of the road and be lost."

He struck a light and drew out his little map, and as he looked before him at the path he saw a great pit filled with mud, which the wicked soldiers had dug just where the pilgrims would have to pass. If they had gone on in the darkness some of them would have been sure to fall into it and might have been smothered before anyone could have drawn them out.

Not far from the pit was another arbor, and in it lay two pilgrims, sleeping soundly. They were lads about Matthew's age, and as Greatheart looked at them he said, "We must try to waken them."

But although he called them by their names, for he knew who they were, they did not hear him, and at last he took them by the shoulders and shook them. This roused them a little, and one of them murmured, "I will pay you when I get some money," and the other said, "I will fight as long as I can hold a sword." Then they settled themselves to sleep again.

Greatheart turned away, for he saw that they could not be awakened.

"What did they mean?" asked Christiana.

"They did not know what they were saying," he answered. "They are in the power of the Wicked Prince, and he will not let them understand their danger until it is too late for them to escape from it."

87

Another Pilgrim

*I*t was now so dark that the pilgrims could scarcely find their way, so they begged Greatheart to light his lantern. With this to guide and cheer them they traveled more comfortably, but the girls and the two little boys were growing very tired, and they began to pray to the King to help them in their weariness.

Presently a cool, fresh breeze sprang up, and as it blew across the plain the air became clearer, and although the moon was still hidden by the clouds, the children could see each other as they walked along.

"Have we nearly crossed the plain?" asked Christiana.

"Not yet," replied Greatheart, "but this is your last night of trouble. Tomorrow we shall reach the Land of Delight, and you will be able to rest there without fear of danger."

"When shall we go into the Celestial City?" asked James.

"I do not know," answered Greatheart. "The King may send for you very soon, or He may give you work to do for Him in the Land of Despair, or He may perhaps send you to help other pilgrims on their journey."

"To be guides, and fight giants, as you have done for us?" asked Joseph eagerly.

"Perhaps, when you are older," said Greatheart, smiling. "But I cannot tell you what the King may think best for you. I only know that you will be happy and that whatever He desires you to do for Him, you will love to do it."

Before the sun rose, while the light was still dim, the pilgrims heard a sound as if someone were speaking not very far from them. They went on quietly, and soon they saw a lad upon his knees by the wayside, with his face turned toward the sky. They knew that he was praying to the King, and as he did not seem to hear their steps they walked slowly, so that they might not disturb him by passing. In a few moments he got up and began to run toward the Celestial City. But Greatheart, seeing that he was a pilgrim, called to him to wait for them.

"Ah!" said old Mr. Honest, when the lad turned round, "I know him!"

"Do you?" asked Valiant. "Who is he?"

"He comes from my own city," replied Honest. "His name is Standfast, and he is one of the King's true pilgrims."

Standfast exclaimed also, when he caught sight of the old man. "What, Father Honest!" he cried. "Are you a pilgrim, too?"

"Yes, indeed," replied Honest.

"It does me good to see you!" said the lad, grasping his hand.

"And it did me good to see you," returned Honest, "seeking the help of your King like a faithful servant."

"Have you been in danger?" asked Valiant, "or were you thanking the King for His mercies?"

"I was in danger," answered Standfast, and then he told his new friends what had happened to him.

88
Folly

You remember how the Flatterer met Christian and Hopeful upon the Enchanted Ground and tried to lead them astray. The Wicked Prince knew that when the pilgrims reached the Land of Delight he would no longer be able to trouble them, so he employed very many of his people in tempting the King's servants while they were upon this plain.

Standfast had been met by a girl whose name was Folly. She was very pretty and had a pleasant way of talking.

"You look very tired," she said to him, "and I am sure you must be lonely. Let me walk with you and be your friend."

But Standfast knew by her gay dress and careless manner that she was not a pilgrim, and he would have nothing to say to her. He walked on silently, and she walked beside him, smiling and saying pleasant things, until at last he grew angry and told her not to trouble him.

When she heard his angry words she laughed and bade him follow her. "I will teach you how to be really happy," she said, "if you will promise to do what I tell you."

But Standfast would not listen to her, and when he found that she was determined not to leave him, he knelt down upon the road and prayed the King to deliver him from her temptations.

"I felt sure the King would help me," said Standfast, "and He did so by letting you overtake me just at the right moment. I did not hear your steps, but the girl must have seen you, for she suddenly turned and went away. Then I thanked the King for His goodness, and I was going to hurry on my way when I heard you call to me."

"I believe I have seen the girl," said Mr. Honest, "or perhaps I have read of her in one of the King's books."

"You may have done both," said Standfast. "She told me her name was Folly."

"Ah!" replied Honest. "She is tall, is she not, and her eyes and hair are dark?"

"Yes," said Standfast.

"She smiles when she speaks, and she has a purse filled with gold fastened to her belt. She is always turning over the money with her fingers as if she loved to touch it."

"Yes, she is just like that."

"I thought I knew something of her. She is a very dangerous enemy."

"Indeed she is," said Greatheart. "Although she is so young, she does more mischief upon the Enchanted Ground than any other of the Wicked Prince's servants. She spends most of her time here, but she is sometimes met with upon the plain near the Wicket-gate, where she calls herself Pleasure and tries to hinder children who are looking for the Way of the King. I could tell you many sad stories of pilgrims who have been deceived by her."

"I saw that she was not a good companion," said Standfast, "but I did not know that I was in such danger."

"Bad companions are always dangerous," replied Greatheart. "You did well to pray to the King, for you would have found it difficult to escape from her."

89

A Happy Morning

*T*he sun had now risen, and as the pilgrims drew near to the borders of the plain, they saw before them in the soft light the beautiful hills which lay above the Dark River. The river itself was not in sight, and they could not yet see the glory of the Celestial City, but they knew that the golden gates were not very far away and that, when they had entered the Land of Delight, all the trouble and danger of their pilgrimage would be over.

"I am glad I came with you!" whispered Mercy, as she slipped her hand into Christiana's. "I have often been very frightened, but now I am quite happy."

"Yes," said Christiana, "we could never have been so happy in our old home."

Then she looked round at her brothers. Matthew had grown taller since his illness, and his face was more thoughtful, but the change in him pleased his sister.

"I think Matthew will be a little like Greatheart in a year or two, don't you?" she said.

"Perhaps the King will give him the same work to do," suggested Mercy.

"To guide the pilgrims? Ah, that is the best work of all. If he could ever be wise enough!"

"Do you think Greatheart was wise at first? He must have been taught, or he could not know so much about the King and His will. And Matthew is so kind and gentle—he would be a good guide."

"Perhaps he would," said Christiana. "He is very brave now that he really loves the King."

The little boys were tired after traveling all night, but the journey had done them good, and their sturdy figures were a pleasant sight. Then Christiana thought of Innocence in the Valley of Peace and wondered how long it would be before the little one came to live with her in the sunny Land of Delight.

All the pilgrims were quiet and thoughtful as they left the plain and followed Greatheart along the sheltered pathways of this beautiful country. Feeble-mind clung closer than ever to the arm of his kind guide, for he was still timid at the sight of strange faces, and when the people of the land saw the pilgrims they came out to welcome them. Mr. Despondency had found a good friend in Valiant, and Much-afraid, though she seldom left her father's side, generally had one of the older girls for her companion. Christiana and Mercy were never far apart, and the two little boys looked upon good-natured old Honest as their special friend. So they took the last steps of their journey together and presently found themselves in one of the King's vineyards, where Greatheart desired them to rest.

"We were so few when we started," said Mercy, as she nestled down upon the soft grass, with her hand clasped in Christiana's. "And now we are quite a large company! Some young and some old, some weak and some strong, and yet the King has cared for us all."

90

In the Land of Delight

*T*he pilgrims were very happy in the Land of Delight. The King's servants provided homes for them all and told them what work they must do. Mr. Despondency and Feeble-mind had only to rest quietly until the King sent for them, but the younger ones had each their own duties to perform.

Christiana spent much of her time in teaching James and Joseph, and she often went with others of the King's servants to welcome the new pilgrims who came into the country nearly every day. Sometimes she stole quietly away with Mercy to walk by the side of the Dark River. The sight of the troubled waters made Mercy tremble, but Christiana always looked beyond them at the beautiful golden light. And at last Mercy began to lose her fear, and she tried to feel as Christiana did, that the coming of the King's messenger would be the beginning of a greater happiness than any she had yet known.

"If only the water were less dark and rough," she used to say, "or if I could have you to cross with me. But if I go alone it will be dreadful!"

"You should not think of the water at all," Christiana always answered. "You should think of the glorious City and the King who lives there, and our dear Prince, and of the Shining Ones who will receive you. Oh, Mercy, you need not be afraid!"

But although her fear grew less, Mercy never liked to watch the river. She loved best to wander in the King's gardens and talk to the children who spent so many hours among the vines and flowers. One duty that the King desired even the tiniest children to perform was the gathering of flowers every day for the older pilgrims, especially for those who were *very* old and weak and not able to walk in the garden and enjoy the beauty and perfume of the growing blossoms.

After a time, when Innocence came to live once more with her sister, Mercy's chief pleasure was to help the little girl in choosing her flowers and carrying them to her friends.

Old Mr. Honest often met them in the gardens in the early morning, and he used to say, "We old pilgrims are very happy, for the little pilgrims strew our way with flowers."

In one of the houses a book was kept in which the King's servants had written the names of many pilgrims who had crossed the river, and the stories of their lives. Matthew and Standfast studied this book very carefully and hoped that the King would some day allow them to fight for Him as bravely as the soldiers of whom they read.

The lame boy, Ready-to-halt, loved the book too, but his favorite stories were those of pilgrims who had been weak and feeble like himself.

"There are so many!" he said one day. "I think it is very comforting to read about them."

And even Mr. Despondency seemed more cheerful when Ready-to-halt came to see him and told him of the King's love for the weak pilgrims—and how the Shining Ones made them their special care.

91

Christiana Crosses
the River

When Greatheart had brought Christiana and her companions safely to their journey's end, he returned to his master's house. But he had promised that he would some day visit them again, for most of his time was spent in guiding pilgrims along the Way of the King.

At last the day came for little Innocence to leave the Valley of Peace, so her kind nurses sent for Greatheart and desired him to take the child safely to her sister. Innocence had learned to love her nurses, but she had not forgotten either Christiana or the young guide. She went with Greatheart quite contentedly, and it would be difficult to say which of the two received the warmer welcome when they reached Christiana's new home.

Greatheart himself was very pleased to see the children again, and he told them that his master had given him permission to stay with them in the Land of Delight for a few weeks, so that he might rest in the King's gardens and prepare himself for future work.

When these weeks of rest were over, it pleased the King to give him some work to do in the Land of Delight. And before this was finished, Christiana and several of the older pilgrims crossed the Dark River and entered the Celestial City.

Christiana and Mercy had often watched the King's messengers as they passed through the streets and wondered at whose house they would knock. When at last a Shining One was seen standing at their own door, the two girls trembled with fear and joy.

But the message was not for Mercy. The Shining One spoke to Christiana.

"Our King calls for you," he said. "He wishes you to come to His Palace."

Christiana felt glad to think of being with the King in His glorious City, but she was sorry to leave her brothers and little Innocence and all her kind friends. However, she knew that it would not be very long before they followed her, and when she remembered this it comforted her.

She thought she would like to bid Greatheart good-bye, so she sent for him and told him what the Shining One had said. He stayed with her a little while, talking about the River and the way of crossing it.

When the other pilgrims heard that Christiana was going away, they came to see her also. She asked Valiant to be a friend to her brothers, and he promised that he would watch over them as long as he remained in that country.

Then she bade them all good-bye, but they would not let her go away alone. They came with her to the water's edge and watched her until she was out of sight. They could see the Shining Ones waiting on the other side, and they knew when Christiana had safely reached the shore, for the bright company moved slowly away from the River up the steep pathway to the golden gates and disappeared at last in the glory of the Celestial City.

Poor little Innocence cried when her sister left her, and so did James and Joseph, but Matthew and Mercy took them home and comforted them.

Greatheart and Valiant could not be sad, although they both loved Christiana dearly. They knew that she had entered the Celestial City and that she would never be weary or anxious anymore. So instead of weeping, they praised the King who had taken His faithful pilgrim to dwell with Him forever.

92

The King Calls
for His Servants

*I*t was not long after the departure of Christiana that a message was brought to the lame boy, Ready-to-halt. Valiant and Greatheart were both with him when the Shining One came, and when he received the King's summons he turned to Valiant saying, "You must keep my crutches until you find another lame pilgrim, and then give them to him with my good wishes, and tell him that I hope he will be able to serve the King better than I have done."

Then he looked at Greatheart and said, "You have been very kind to me, and you have helped me wonderfully in my pilgrimage."

His two friends went with him to the brink of the River, and when he had stepped into the water, he laid his crutches down upon the bank.

"I shall never need them again!" he said. "I know that in the King's City there are horses and chariots which shine like the sun."

A few days later Feeble-mind was sent for. The King's message to him was very kind and gentle, and the poor, weak pilgrim rejoiced to think that he would soon be in a land where toil and trouble are unknown.

Some weeks passed away before the Shining Ones came again, and their next message was for Mr. Despondency. When Much-afraid heard it, she begged to go with him, and the King, who knew how dearly she loved her father and how faithful she had been to him through all the dangers and difficulties of their pilgrimage, granted her request. So the father and daughter entered the Dark River hand in hand, and the pilgrims upon the shore could hear Much-afraid singing a song of praise as she went through the water, although she was too far away for them to distinguish its words.

Old Mr. Honest received the next summons, and just at that time the River was so full of water that it overflowed its banks. But although it seemed terribly wide and deep, the good old man was not afraid. He knew that his King would not allow him to perish in the dark waters. He went cheerfully down to the shore at the appointed time, and there he found a friend waiting for him—a man whom he had known nearly all his life, whose name was Good-conscience.

He had once said to him, "I shall hope to have your help when I cross the Dark River." And Good-Conscience had remembered this and had obtained the King's leave to help his friend in this last hour of trouble. So he gave him his hand. And although the waters raged wildly around them, Honest leaned upon his strong shoulders and crossed the River in safety.

93

The Departure of Valiant and Standfast

*T*he same messenger who called Mr. Honest summoned Valiant also, but he went over the River later in the day. He had no fear of the crossing, for he had always been brave, and his heart was full of trust in the good King. He was longing to see his wife and his dear little son once more, and he knew how happy Christian and his mother would be when they heard who was waiting to receive their welcome.

"Mine has been a hard pilgrimage," he said, "and I have had to fight my way through many troubles and dangers. But I am going now to my true home in the Celestial City, where I shall be safe and happy forever."

The good soldier had no longer any use for his sword, so he left the bright weapon in Greatheart's care and desired him to give it to some other pilgrim. Then he entered the River, and his friends soon lost sight of him; but presently

the sound of the silver trumpets was heard upon the other shore, and they knew that Valiant was on his way to the gates of the City.

I can only tell you of the departure of one more pilgrim. Standfast had hoped that he might be allowed to spend a long life in working for the King, but this was not his Master's will. The King had need of His faithful young servant in the Celestial City, and very soon he was summoned to cross the River.

At first Standfast could scarcely believe that the King really wished to receive him into His own Palace, but the Shining One assured him that it was true.

"You have served my Master very faithfully," said he, "and He is not willing that you should be living at a distance from Him any longer."

So Standfast prepared for his last journey and gave Greatheart many messages, for he hoped that the guide would perhaps some day meet with others of his family who might be following in his steps. The floods had gone down before this time, and the water was very still and calm. When Standfast reached the middle of the River, he turned and spoke once more to his friends.

"This River makes so many people afraid!" said he. "Indeed, I was frightened myself before I entered it. But my fear is gone. I can feel the firm ground under my feet, and very soon I shall be with my Prince. It has been very pleasant to hear of Him and think of Him, but now I shall see Him with my own eyes. He has helped me and strengthened me all through my pilgrimage, and He is with me now."

Then the other pilgrims saw that, as he turned again toward the City, a beautiful light fell upon his face. And in the clear air they could see quite across the River and were able to watch the multitude of Shining Ones who came down to receive the faithful lad and lead him into the presence of the King.